Math GAMES

for Middle School

Challenges and Skill-Builders for Students at Every Level

MARIO SALVADORI

and Joseph P. Wright

CHICAGO REVIEW PRESS

Library of Congress Cataloging-in-Publication Data

Salvadori, Mario George, 1907–1997
    Math games for middle school : challenges and skill-builders for students at
every level / Mario Salvadori and Joseph P. Wright.
        p. cm.
    Summary: Uses explanations, word problems, and games to cover some
mathematical topics that middle school students need to know, including the
invention of numerical notations, basic arithmetical operations, measurements,
geometry, graphs, and probability.
    ISBN 1–55652–288–6 (alk. paper)
    1. Mathematics—Study and teaching (Middle school) 2. Games in mathe-
matics education. [1. Mathematics. 2. Mathematics—Problems, exercises, etc.]
I. Wright Joseph P. 1939–   . II. Title.
QA135.5.S233   1998
510'.71'2—dc21   97–51422
                                                                                  CIP
                                                                                  AC

Published by Chicago Review Press, Incorporated
814 N. Franklin Street
Chicago, Illinois 60610

ISBN 1-55652-288-6

Printed in the United States of America

To Maia and Daniel, who discovered big numbers at age two.

Preface

This book was written

Because I hated math in school and it took a Ph.D. to make me love it;

Because math is as beautiful as poetry and as useful as water;

Because children are not retarded adults; while, sometimes, adults behave like retarded children;

Because in our country even intelligent people boast that they hate mathematics and they will never understand it.

and

To make it easier for teachers to teach math and for students to learn it;

To show our students that math is a fascinating human invention;

To satisfy the growing demand of our culture for more and more advanced math, science, and technology;

And finally

To thank all my students, from kindergarten to Ph.D.s, who for 64 years have given me the joy of explaining to them what mathematics really is.

—Mario Salvadori

Acknowledgments

I wish to express my deep gratitude to:

Joe Wright, a first-rate mathematician and real friend who has read the typescript of this book, patiently prepared the solutions for the problems in each Math Camp, and done all the illustrations on the computer. I hereby thank him for his help and exonerate him for any and all mistakes due to me.

My wife Carol, who translated my English-Italian into pure American.

Dr. Lorraine Whitman, the executive director of the Salvadori Educational Center, for her editorial help.

Mr. Bennett Viseltear for his editorial suggestions and his patience in typing the early versions of this book.

Linda Matthews, master editor, and her able staff at Chicago Review Press, for their skill and dedication.

Tracey Wright, curriculum developer at TERC, Cambridge, Massachusetts, for her editorial help.

Ms. Caroline Daviews, mathematics teacher, and Mrs. Evelyn Wiesfield, director of the Booker T. Washington Minischool, and Mr. Jules Linden, the superb principal of the Booker T. Washington Magnet School 54 in District 3 of the New York City Board of Education, for their support of my lectures in their school for many terms.

And last but not least, the sixth- and seventh-grade students of the Booker T. Washington Minischool for their enthusiasm and their creative suggestions.

Contents

Chapter One

The Invention of Numbers 1

What Happened 20,000 Years Ago   1
Abstraction   2
Counting   2
International Counting Symbols   3
Positional Shorthand   4
Exponential Shorthand   5
Math Camp 1   6
The Binary Number System   7
Math Camp 2   9

Chapter Two

**Adding, Multiplying,
Subtracting, and Dividing Numbers**   11

Addition   11
Math Camp 3   12
Multiplication   13
Math Camp 4   14
Subtraction   15
Math Camp 5   17
Division   18
Math Camp 6   21

Chapter Three

More Operations on Numbers   23

The Number Line   23
Math Camp 7   25
Exponents   26
Math Camp 8   28
Roots   29
Math Camp 9   31
Fractions   32
Operations on Fractions   33
Math Camp 10   37

Working with Negative Numbers   39
Math Camp 11   42
Estimating and Rounding Off   44
Math Camp 12   46

Chapter Four

Measurements   49

What Is Measuring?   49
Math Camp 13   51
The SI System   52
How to Get Used to the SI System   54
Math Camp 14   55

Chapter Five

Plane Geometry   57

The Circle   57
Math Camp 15   63
The Triangle   66
Math Camp 16   71
The Quadrilaterals   73
Math Camp 17   74
The Regular Polygons   76
Math Camp 18   77

Chapter Six

Space Geometry   79

Our Space   79
Space Figures Generated by Plane Figures   79
Math Camp 19   82
Polyhedra   83
Math Camp 20   84

Chapter Seven

The Art of Graphing   89

Bar Graphs   89
Straight Lines in the Cartesian Plane   90
Curved Graphs   93
The Asymetric Approach to π 95
The Concept of Scale   97
Math Camp 21   99

Chapter Eight

Simultaneous Linear Equations   103

Two Questions and Two Answers   103
Math Camp 22   104

Chapter Nine

Permutations And Combinations   107

Permutations and Combinations   107
The Birthday Party   107
The Pizza Shop   108
Repeating Yourself   110
Using the Words of Mathematicians   110
The U.S. Alpine Club   112
The Graduation Prom   114
Sitting in Class   114
Math Camp 23   116

Chapter Ten

The Mathematics of Chance   119

Throwing Pennies   119
Playing Lotto   122
The Car License-Plate Game   122
Shooting Craps (the Simple Way)   124
Math Camp 24   126

Answers

Answers to Math Camps   129

Index   165

Introduction

This book is the result of my own education and teaching experience, both rather unusual.

For the last 20 years I have taught in New York City and indirectly (through the materials of the Salvadori Center) all over the United States and in some foreign countries. The Salvadori Center is dedicated to improving teaching in middle schools, with particular emphasis on math and science (though its methodology is applicable to all subjects). So far, The Salvadori Center has reached over 120,000 students in New York City alone, dramatically reducing the dropout rate from the 40%-plus common in our town.

Prior to my interest in the public schools, I taught on the faculties of Columbia University for 50 years and Princeton University for five years. And, at the beginning of my university career, I was on the faculty of the University of Rome, my native city, for eight years.

My Italian education ended with one doctorate in mathematical physics and another in civil engineering. My 50-year professional career in the United States was dedicated to structural engineering design and to consultation in applied mechanics problems. I have dedicated the last years of my life entirely to teaching the young, from kindergartners through high schoolers.

I dedicate this book to all the wonderful teachers and students it has been my good fortune to meet in our schools. On the basis of this experience, I am eager to share my pedagogical approach to teaching. It consists of these elementary rules:

I teach young students with the same respect I taught Ph.D. students.

I present the curriculum, whatever the subject, through realistic examples from the students' own world.

Whenever possible, I get the students interested by means of hands-on work involving easily built models.

I ask to be called "Mario" and to be interrupted whenever one of my statements is not clearly understood by anyone in class, having discovered that respect comes from appreciation rather than from authority, and that what is not clear to one student, most of the time is not clear to many.

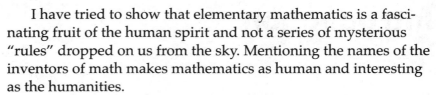

I have tried to show that elementary mathematics is a fascinating fruit of the human spirit and not a series of mysterious "rules" dropped on us from the sky. Mentioning the names of the inventors of math makes mathematics as human and interesting as the humanities.

Although Italian by birth and education, I have not considered the study of Roman numerals essential to the education of American students. And, although a scientist, I have not considered it necessary to deal with some of the higher concepts of mathematics in middle school.

I have tried to satisfy the sixth-grade requirements of the Board of Education of New York City, which are similar to those of most boards of education in the United States.

I hope my colleagues in middle schools will have as much fun teaching mathematics according to these tried rules as I have had in teaching both the elementary and the advanced concepts of math.

Good luck!

—Mario Salvadori

Postscript

This book is just one of several projects that Mario was working on when he died in June of 1997 at the age of 90. On several occasions, usually when we met to discuss the book, he asked me the same question he liked to ask his students, "Are you having fun?" I naturally said yes, both because I enjoy mathematics and I enjoyed being with him.

Mario thought of math as a game—something to have fun with—and he always tried to communicate that sense of play to his "kids." He chose the name of this book for that reason. He knew the importance of mathematics and he wanted to present, in as entertaining a way as he could, some challenging material that should be part of a typical middle-school student's training. I think he succeeded admirably.

—Joe Wright
9/12/97

Chapter 1

The Invention of Numbers

 WHAT HAPPENED 20,000 YEARS AGO

Astronomers, the scientists who study the sky, tell us that our universe, with all its billions and billions of stars, was born in a tremendous explosion that they call the Big Bang, about 15 billion years ago (that's 15 followed by nine zeros!). They also tell us that the sun and our earth were born about 5 billion years ago. Recently, anthropologists—the scientists who study humankind—discovered evidence that we human beings appeared for the first time on the surface of the earth about 4 million years ago.

As you can see, it all started a long, long time ago. Yet math was invented only about 20,000 years ago, the day some genius among our ancestors realized that three stars, three stones, three trees, and three children had something in common: the property of "three-ness"! To record this great discovery, this brightest of people held up three fingers or cut three notches on a tree branch with a sharp stone.

Although we were not there to see it, I am quite sure that our bright ancestor got so excited at this discovery that he or she began counting everything, just as you did when you first discovered that you had one, then two, then three, four, and five fingers on each hand.

Actually, our language gives us fairly good evidence that our ancestors also counted on their fingers. The numbers from 0 to 9 are sometimes called "digits" in English, and the word "digit" comes from "digitus," the Latin word for finger. Whether numbers were "discovered" or "invented" is harder to say. I believe they were invented by people, as was the rest of mathematics, starting about 20,000 years ago.

ABSTRACTION

The idea of numbers is an **abstract** idea, meaning a thought in our minds about something that may not even exist. For example, we can think of a green cow with five legs, although real cows have only four legs and are not green. As people kept inventing more and more mathematical ideas, math kept becoming more and more abstract and, at the same time, more and more useful. The trouble is that many of us are not very good at abstract thinking. We find the abstractions of math difficult if not impossible to understand, and we end up hating mathematics.

If any of my readers are among the "abstract math haters," I have good news for them. The idea of numbers may be abstract, but numbers are extremely useful because they represent very real things. We use mathematics so often, every day of our lives, that we could not live without it. Just think of this: could you buy anything at a store if you could not use numbers to count?

Of course, as you already know, math goes beyond mere counting. You are living at a time when science influences every aspect of our lives. We could not fly without the mathematical science of aerodynamics needed to build airplanes; your doctor could not treat you when you are sick without the mathematics of chemistry needed to make pills; nor could you talk with your friends over the phone or look at television without the mathematics of electronics. In short, whether we like it or not, you and I must use math all the time. And we live better than our early ancestors because more and more math is being invented every day to make our lives healthier, easier, and more pleasant.

Let us now find out how mathematics was invented, beginning with counting. I bet you that by the time you finish this book, you will agree with me about what mathematics really is— a fascinating game that anybody can enjoy playing as well as a needed game that we all must play for our own good.

COUNTING

Our early ancestors may have held up the fingers of their hands or cut notches like / / / on tree branches to indicate how many cows they had in the corral or how many apples they had picked that day. But they must have soon realized that no tree branch could be long enough to count a very large number of cows or apples. They eventually invented names for groups of notches and, since we don't know what language they spoke, we might as well imagine that they spoke English and said "one" for /, "two" for //, "three" for ///, or "nine" for /////////, and so on. Thus did special words become useful substitutes for notches.

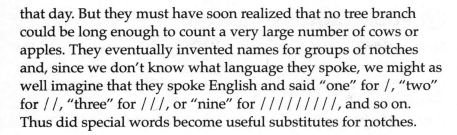 INTERNATIONAL COUNTING SYMBOLS

Our ancestors had an easy time using their special words to communicate with the members of their own tribe, but they soon realized that these words were not understood by members of tribes with which they wished to exchange goods, because they spoke a different language. We would have the same problem today. How could we sell 10 cars to a Spanish car dealer by using the word "ten" when 10 in Spanish is "diez"?

This problem was solved in due time by substituting **numerals**, more easily recognized **shorthand** symbols for the special words.

The word "shorthand" comes from a kind of special writing where symbols substitute for letters, words, and phrases, allowing people to write so fast that they can put a speech on paper while it is being delivered. For example, all the speeches of our congressmen and congresswomen in the House of Representatives are taken down in shorthand. To make the writing easier, typewriters are made that have shorthand symbols instead of letters.

Math is another kind of shorthand language that has grown easier and easier to use by becoming shorter and shorter. In math shorthand, at least in Europe, "one" became 1, "two" became 2, "three" became 3, "nine" became 9, and so on, in imitation of the numerals that were brought to Europe from India by the Arabs, many centuries ago. Nowadays the numerals 1, 2, 3, 4, and so on are called the Hindu-Arabic numerals (or simply the Arabic numerals), as a way of recognizing the importance of this contribution to mathematics.

Unfortunately the problem of communicating with numerals among all the people of the world has not been solved yet, because not all countries have adopted the same symbols. Yet more and more countries are doing so today. For example, although the Japanese language has its own numerals, the Japanese have adopted the Hindu-Arabic numerals for their telephone numbers. Hopefully, these numerals will soon be used internationally.

POSITIONAL SHORTHAND

So far, so good. Our nine numerals from 1 to 9 work very well if we never have to count more than nine objects, but can you imagine how tough it would be to invent and memorize numerals for every number bigger than nine? Actually it would be impossible, because there is no limit to how high you can count. There is no largest number, nor is there a smallest number!

We must be grateful to the Hindus of India for the solution of this difficult counting problem and particularly to the Hindu mathematician Bhaskara, who published the complete solution to the problem in 1150 A.D. It was already known at the time that one more numeral was needed for counting all possible numbers, a numeral the Hindus called "sunya" (meaning "empty"), and we call "zero." (With zero we can make the mathematical statement: "I have zero apples," instead of the verbal statement: "I have no apples.") Bhaskara suggested that all numbers, large or small as they might be, could be represented by the sum of a sequence of numerals chosen among the ten symbols 0 to 9, called digits, by simply positioning them to the left or to the right of a **decimal dot**. Those to the left of the dot are understood to be multiplied by increasing powers of 10 and those to the right of the dot are understood to be divided by increasing powers of 10, depending on their distance from the decimal dot, according to the following rules: "The first digit to the left of the dot is to be multiplied by 1, the next digit to its left by 10, the next by 10×10, the next by $10 \times 10 \times 10$, and so on. The first digit to the right of the decimal dot is to be divided by 10, the next to its right divided by 10×10, the next by $10 \times 10 \times 10$, and so on."

For example, the Bhaskara number 234.567 represents:

$$2 \times 10 \times 10 + 3 \times 10 + 4 \times 1 + 5/10 + 6/(10 \times 10) + 7/(10 \times 10 \times 10)$$
$$= 2 \times 100 + 3 \times 10 + 4 \times 1 + 5/10 + 6/100 + 7/1000$$

as shown in Table 1.

You may read this as "Two hundreds, three tens, four ones, five tenths, six hundredths, and seven thousandths."

This simple way of representing any number by means of the ten digits 0 to 9 is called "the Hindu-Arabic system of number representation" or simply the **decimal** system, because it is based on the powers of 10.

You may be interested to know that, while Bhaskara gave the first complete explanation of the Hindu-Arabic representation system in 1150 A.D., the Mayas of Central America had their own

Table 1

Hundreds	Tens	Ones	Dot	Tenths	Hundredths	Thousandths
2	3	4	.	5	6	7

number system, which included the number zero, in the fourth century A.D., about 750 years before Bhaskara!

🎲 EXPONENTIAL SHORTHAND

As you will learn in Section 2 of Chapter Three, multiplication of the same number, say 10, by itself, say 6 times, may be represented by the **exponential** shorthand symbol 10^6 where 6 is called the **exponent** and 10 is called the **base.** Any number n (other than zero) with 0 as the exponent represents the digit 1, or $n^0 = 1$. Similarly, any number, say 5, divided 3 times by any other number, say 7, may be represented by the negative exponential; thus $5/(7 \times 7 \times 7) = 5 \times 7^{-3}$. By means of these exponential shorthand symbols, the decimal positional representation of the number 234.567 can be written:

$$2 \times 10^2 + 3 \times 10^1 + 4 \times 10^0 + 5 \times 10^{-1} + 6 \times 10^{-2} + 7 \times 10^{-3}.$$

Decimal notation is particularly easy to use because powers of 10 are easy to remember. For example:

$$10^4 = 10,000; \quad 10^3 = 1,000; \quad 10^2 = 100; \quad 10^1 = 10;$$
$$10^0 = 1; \quad 10^{-1} = 1/10; \quad 10^{-2} = 1/100; \quad 10^{-3} = 1/1,000;$$
$$10^{-4} = 1/10,000; \quad \text{and so on.}$$

Since you are going to use numbers every single day of your life, you should become familiar with them and use them with the same facility with which you might hit a baseball or shoot a basketball. Practice with the following games in Math Camp 1. You might have fun playing the games with a friend and competing against one another to see who gets the correct solution first.

1 Write the following numbers in the decimal representation system:

>   Three hundred fifty;
>
>   Four thousand nine hundred twenty-five;
>
>   One million, two hundred thousand, three hundred forty-five.

2 Write the following numbers in English:

>   421.25;
>
>   42,375.374;
>
>   21,300,750,221.045.

3 Write the following numbers as the sum of their components in powers of 10:

>   321;
>
>   254,321.456;
>
>   500,401,302,002.

4 Write the following numbers in their decimal representations:

$$5 \times 10^3 + 0 \times 10^2 + 3 \times 10 + 4;$$
$$6 \times 10^9 + 5 \times 10^7 + 2 \times 10^5;$$
$$3 \times 10^4 + 2 \times 10^2 + 5.$$

5 Write the following numbers in their decimal representations:

$$2 \times 10^2 + 3 \times 10 + 4 \times 10^0 + 3 \times 10^{-1} + 5 \times 10^{-2};$$
$$4 \times 10^{-1} + 5 \times 10^{-2} + 6 \times 10^{-3};$$
$$1 \times 10^4 + 2 \times 10^3 + 4 \times 10^{-1} + 6 \times 10^{-2}.$$

THE BINARY NUMBER SYSTEM

You learned in Section 6 that it is efficient and convenient to express numbers by their location to the left and the right of the decimal dot, with the understanding that their position implies multiplication by the exponential powers of 10. For example, the number 312.54 is the positional decimal representation of:

$$3 \times 10^2 + 1 \times 10^1 + 2 \times 10^0 + 5 \times 10^{-1} + 4 \times 10^{-2}$$
$$= 300 + 10 + 2 + 0.5 + 0.04 = 312.54$$

On the other hand, there are situations where it is more convenient to represent a number with a base other than 10. The **binary** number system uses the powers of 2 and just two numerals, 1 and 0 (rather than all ten numerals, 0 to 9, of the decimal system). Binary numbers are essential for electronic computers because computers are actually just a bunch of switches that can only be on or off, and these two conditions are conveniently represented by two numerals, 1 (for on) and 0 (for off).

Table 2 gives the binary representations of the decimal numbers from 0 to 10 in the second row.

Table 2

0	1	2	3	4	5	6	7	8	9	10
0	1	10	11	100	101	110	111	1000	1001	1010

Let us see an example of binary representation by expressing powers of 2 exponentially and using 1 or 0 to indicate the number of times each power of 2 must be taken. Table 3 has all the information needed to do this.

Table 3

32	16	8	4	2	1		1/2	1/4	1/8	1/16	1/32
2^5	2^4	2^3	2^2	2^1	2^0		2^{-1}	2^{-2}	2^{-3}	2^{-4}	2^{-5}
1	0	1	0	0	1	.	1	1	0	0	1

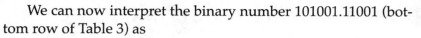

We can now interpret the binary number 101001.11001 (bottom row of Table 3) as

$$1 \times 2^5 + 0 \times 2^4 \times 1 \times 2^3 + 0 \times 2^2 + 0 \times 2^1 \times 1 \times 2^0 + 1 \times 2^{-1} + 1 \times 2^{-2}$$
$$+ 0 \times 2^{-3} + 0 \times 2^{-4} + 1 \times 2^{-5}.$$

Remembering that any nonzero number to the power 0 means 1, this is

$$1 \times 32 + 0 \times 16 + 1 \times 8 + 0 \times 4 + 0 \times 2 + 1 \times 1 + 1 \times 1/2 + 1 \times 1/4$$
$$+ 0 \times 1/8 + 0 \times 1/16 + 1 \times 1/32,$$

or, in the decimal representation,

$$32 + 8 + 1 + 1/2 + 1/4 + 1/32 = 41.78125.$$

You realize, of course, that the representation of a number in the binary system is usually much longer than that in the decimal system. For example, in Table 2, the single decimal number 9 requires four binary digits. And in our example just above, the decimal number 41.78125 has seven decimal digits but its binary representation, 101001.11001, has eleven binary digits. Nonetheless, since a computer is really just a bunch of switches, each of which is either on or off, it is cheaper to have these switches represent binary numbers (off = 0, on = 1) than to have them represent decimal digits.

Let us now translate a decimal number into a binary number:

$$21.75 = 2 \times 10 + 1 \times 1 + 7 \times 10^{-1} + 5 \times 10^{-2}$$

16	8	4	2	1		1/2	1/4	1/8	1/16
2^4	2^3	2^2	2^1	2^0		2^{-1}	2^{-2}	2^{-3}	2^{-4}
1	0	1	0	1	.	1	1	0	0

$$= 1 \times 16 + 1 \times 4 + 1 \times 1 + 1 \times 0.5 + 1 \times 0.25$$
$$= 16 + 4 + 1 + 0.5 + 0.25 = 21.75$$

Math ⚜ Camp 2

1 Translate the following decimals into binary numbers:

      21;

      248.625;

      2,003,481;

      0.3125.

2 Translate the following binary numbers into decimal notation and then do the indicated operations (if any):

      1010;

      11001;

      $1100 + 011$;

      $1010 + 101 - 10$;

      $111 + 1010 - 11$;

      1001×110.

Chapter 2

Adding, Multiplying, Subtracting, and Dividing Numbers

■ ADDITION

Let us assume that you bought two pairs of blue socks and three pairs of red socks. To find out how many pairs of socks you bought, you could do what our ancestors did (and children still do): you could count by ones on the fingers of your hands and say:

"(One and one) and (one and one and one) pairs of socks is five pairs of socks."

But mathematicians have invented a shorthand operation for this long way of counting. It is represented by the symbol + (plus) and is called **addition.** So, we write the long count of our ancestors simply as:

$$2 + 3 = 5.$$

Of course, as we talked about in Chapter One, you will really appreciate the advantage of using the Hindu-Arabic or decimal number system when you have to perform the addition of large numbers, or the addition of a large number of numbers.

Notice that addition has the property of being **commutative;** that is, the **sum** of adding two or more numbers is independent of the order in which they are added:

$$7 + 1 + 4 = (7 + 1) + 4 = (1 + 4) + 7 = (4 + 1) + 7 = 12.$$

Suppose you bought two baskets of apples, one with 29 and the other with 37 apples. How many apples did you buy altogether?

When adding in the decimal representation, it is advisable to add the numbers vertically, spelling out the numbers multiplied by the increasing powers of 10. For example, in adding 29 to 37, write 29 as 20 + 9 and 37 as 30 + 7. Then add the unit numbers 9 + 7 = 16, and write 16 as 10 + 6. Continuing in this manner, the addition 29 + 37 becomes:

$$\begin{array}{r} 29 \\ 37 \\ \hline ? \end{array} \quad = \quad \begin{array}{r} 20 + 9 \\ + 30 + 7 \\ \hline 50 + 16 = 50 + 10 + 6 \end{array} \quad = \quad 60 + 6 = 66.$$

Once you have become familiar with the decimal number representation, addition can be shorthanded by putting the 1 from 10 + 6, which comes from 9 + 7 = 16, above the tens column and simplifying the writing to:

$$\begin{array}{r} 1 \\ 29 \\ 37 \\ \hline 66 \end{array}$$

The following example illustrates this shorthand writing of addition with more and bigger numbers:

$$\begin{array}{r} 1\ 12 \\ 3{,}456.21 \\ 2{,}229.02 \\ 375.15 \\ \hline 6{,}060.38 \end{array}$$

———— Math ⚘ Camp ————
3

1 **Perform the following additions:**
479 + 237;   1,245 + 2,377;   10,003,700 + 2,549;
$3.75 + $2.99 + $4.75 + $0.35 + $1.01;
25,432 miles + 32,567 miles + 298,000 miles + 12,354 miles.

2 You bought three dolls for your sisters: one for $2.75, another for $3.94, and the third for $4.58. How much did you spend?

3 On Sunday you went to the movies for $3.50, bought popcorn for $0.99, took the bus to the movies for $1.20, and went back home on the subway for $0.90. How much did Sunday cost you?

4 You are training for a race and run the following number of miles each day for a week:

Day	Mon	Tue	Wed	Thu	Fri	Sat	Sun
Miles	3.5	3.0	2.7	4.0	2.8	5.0	5.0

How many miles did you run that week?

5 During a vacation trip you flew 3,400 miles the first day, 2,500 miles the fifth day, and 3,450 miles the last day. How many miles did you fly during the trip?

6 You had $20,235.55 in your bank account and deposited $1,200.00 in the bank on Monday, $4,519.00 on Tuesday, $245.00 on Wednesday, and $345.60 on Friday. How much money do you have in your account on Saturday?

⚅ MULTIPLICATION

You ran three miles a day for a week to train for a race. How many miles did you run during that training week?

If you had just learned the operation of addition, I believe you would probably have answered this question by adding three miles, over and over, seven times:

$$3 + 3 + 3 + 3 + 3 + 3 + 3 = 21 \text{ mi.}$$

But mathematicians have invented a shorthand operation, called **multiplication,** and represent it by the symbol $\times$ ("times") or sometimes by a dot $\cdot$. Multiplication can be used whenever one must add the same number many times. In the example we are discussing, using the symbol $\times$, one would simply write:

$$7 \times 3 = 21$$

and read the line as: "Seven times three equals twenty-one" to indicate that the same number, 3, has been added 7 times. The first number of the multiplication is called the **multiplier,** the second the **multiplicand,** and the result of the multiplication the **product.**

Since the symbol × looks a lot like the letter x, and since the letter x is often used in mathematics to represent the value of an unknown number (called the unknown), a dot is used as the multiplication symbol whenever there might be a confusion between the two. Thus one can write: $3 \times 2 = 6$ or $3 \cdot 2 = 6$. They mean the same thing.

Because multiplication is a shorthand symbol for summation, or adding, it is also commutative, meaning the order of multiplication does not matter:

$$3 \times 5 \times 7 = (7 \times 3) \times 5 = (7 \times 5) \times 3 = 105.$$

If you want to see the commutative property of multiplication, set six apples on three plates, two apples per plate; then set the same six apples on two plates, three apples per plate.

In order to become skillful at multiplication you must memorize the products of (at least) the numbers 0 through 12 in all possible combinations. These are shown in Table 4—the multiplication table. If you can memorize the products of numbers larger than those given in that table, you will be even better off when dealing with multiplication. If you do not know Table 4 already, it is absolutely essential that you start memorizing it right now. It is the only real memorization you need in elementary math.

—————— Math 🌵 Camp ——————
4

1 John has four married brothers, three married sisters, and six unmarried cousins. His parents invite them all for Christmas and give their children and their spouses gifts costing $20 each, and their nephews and nieces gifts costing $15 each. How much do John's parents spend on Christmas gifts? (Assume John to be unmarried.)

2 A river flows at a speed of 3 miles per hour over its first 30 miles, twice as fast over its second 20 miles, and three times as fast during the last 10 miles. At what speed does the river flow in the last 10 miles?

Table 4   Multiplication Table

x	0	1	2	3	4	5	6	7	8	9	10	11	12
0	0	0	0	0	0	0	0	0	0	0	0	0	0
1	0	1	2	3	4	5	6	7	8	9	10	11	12
2	0	2	4	6	8	10	12	14	16	18	20	22	24
3	0	3	6	9	12	15	18	21	24	27	30	33	36
4	0	4	8	12	16	20	24	28	32	36	40	44	48
5	0	5	10	15	20	25	30	35	40	45	50	55	60
6	0	6	12	18	24	30	36	42	48	54	60	66	72
7	0	7	14	21	28	35	42	49	56	63	70	77	84
8	0	8	16	24	32	40	48	56	64	72	80	88	96
9	0	9	18	27	36	45	54	63	72	81	90	99	108
10	0	10	20	30	40	50	60	70	80	90	100	110	120
11	0	11	22	33	44	55	66	77	88	99	110	121	132
12	0	12	24	36	48	60	72	84	96	108	120	132	144

3 A soccer player receives the ball at a speed of 25 miles per hour and passes it twice as fast to a player who kicks it into the goal one and one-half times faster than that, scoring a goal. At what speed is the ball kicked into the goal?

🎲 SUBTRACTION

Let us assume that your school year lasts 184 days. So far you have gone to school 72 days and are looking forward to summer vacation. How many more days do you still have to go to school?

Let us call x the number of days you must still go to school. (In mathematics, "unknowns" are often indicated by one of the last letters of the alphabet, like x, y, or z.) What we know about x is that the sum of x and 72 must add up to 184. In mathematical symbols,

$$72 + x = 184.$$

■ ■ ■ ■

This relationship of equality is called an **equation,** and you may look at it as a balance (Fig. 1).

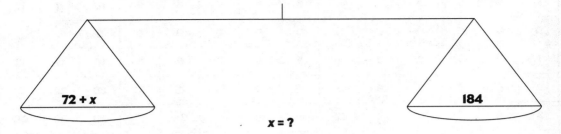

Figure 1 An equation is like a balance. The amount of weight on each side must be the same to maintain equilibrium. Therefore, $x = 112$.

This equation states: "The sum of 72 plus x on the left side of the equal sign (=) is equal to the number 184 on the right side of the equal sign." (The equal sign was invented in the 16th century by a British mathematician who said, "Nothing could be more equal than two little line segments parallel to each other and of equal length.")

If you take away or add the same weight on both sides of a balance, you do not disturb the equilibrium of the balance. Similarly, if you take away (subtract, as we say in math) or add the same number on both sides of an equation, the equation is still true. Subtracting 72 from both sides of our equation, we obtain:

$$72 - 72 + x = 184 - 72 = 112,$$

or

$$x = 112,$$

which tells you that you still have 112 days to go to school.

The operation of subtraction, represented by the symbol – (minus), is the opposite of the operation of addition: subtraction takes away while addition adds. It is performed vertically, very much like addition, but by taking away from the larger number (the **minuend**) the smaller number (the **subtrahend**) to obtain the **difference.** For example:

$$
\begin{array}{r}
345 \text{ (the minuend)} \\
-121 \text{ (the subtrahend)} \\
\hline
224. \text{ (the difference)}
\end{array}
$$

In addition, you may have to add ones from column to column going left. Similarly, in subtraction, you may have to "borrow" ones from the left when a digit of the minuend is smaller than that of the subtrahend. For example, when subtracting 275 from 341 you write:

$$
\begin{array}{r}
{-1}{+10} \\
{-1}{+10} \\
341 \\
{-2}75 \\
\hline
066
\end{array}
$$

Even if, at first, subtraction feels a little more difficult than addition, it can be checked easily by addition. To check that $341 - 275 = 66$, all you have to do is add 66 to 275:

$$
\begin{array}{r}
66 \\
+275 \\
\hline
341
\end{array}
$$

Thus, you see that your subtraction was correct.
(See Section 1 of Chapter Three to learn the consequence of subtracting a larger subtrahend from a smaller minuend.)

Math Camp 5

1 You had $3,429 in your bank account and withdrew $1,307 from it on Monday. How much do you have left in the account?

2 You had $5,000 in your bank account and withdrew $1,409 on Monday, $517 on Tuesday, and $2,098 on Wednesday. How much money do you have left in your account?

3 An outdoor thermometer shows a temperature of 95°F at noon and 48°F at 9 p.m. By how many degrees Fahrenheit did the temperature decrease between noon and 9 p.m.?

(The symbol °F after the two numbers 95 and 48 shows that the temperature is measured in **Fahrenheit degrees** on the Fahrenheit scale, which is used to measure temperature in the United States and Britain. On the Fahrenheit scale, the freezing temperature of water is 32°F and the boiling temperature of water is 212°F. For more about temperature, see Chapter Four.)

4 You drive 470 miles from Albany, NY, to Washington, D.C., passing through New York City. The distance between New York City and Washington, D.C. is 220 miles. What is the distance between Albany and New York City?

5 Your school has 900 students in sixth, seventh, and eighth grades. On Monday, 12 students call in sick in sixth grade, 15 in seventh grade, and 21 in eighth grade. How many students attended school on Monday?

6 George Washington was born in 1732 and died in 1799. How old was he when he died?

7 This morning, you spent $10.75 for meat, $4.50 for fruit, $6.52 for butter, and $2.25 for bread. You paid with a $50.00 bill. How much change did you get?

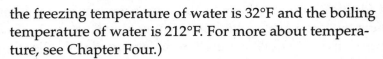 DIVISION

Let us assume that you bought a remnant of material for $25.00 at $6.25 a yard. How many yards of material did you buy? If you had just learned subtraction, I have a hunch you might try to use it to find the answer to this problem by subtracting $6.25 from $25.00 until you ended up with a zero:

$$\$25.00 - \$6.25 - \$6.25 - \$6.25 - \$6.25 = 0.$$

You would have been lucky this time: $6.25 fits exactly four times into $25.00. So you bought four yards of material. Just as multiplication was invented as a shorthand operation for the repeated addition of equal numbers, mathematicians have invented a shorthand operation for the repeated subtraction of equal numbers, called **division**. Division actually does more than simply subtracting numbers quickly. It also finds out exactly how many times a number, called the **divisor**, fits into another number, called the **dividend**. The number of times the divisor fits into the dividend is called the **quotient**.

Division is expressed in shorthand by any of the following four symbols:

$$\div \quad - \quad \overline{)} \quad /$$

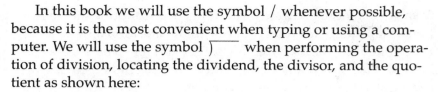

In this book we will use the symbol / whenever possible, because it is the most convenient when typing or using a computer. We will use the symbol $\overline{)}$ when performing the operation of division, locating the dividend, the divisor, and the quotient as shown here:

$$\text{divisor}\overline{)\text{dividend}}^{\text{quotient}}$$

In the example of the material remnant we would write:

$$6.25\overline{)25.00,}^{4}$$

indicating that we divided 25.00 by 6.25, finding 4 as our quotient.

The following example illustrates step by step how division gives the successive digits of the quotient by dividing the dividend by the successive digits of the divisor:

$$\text{divisor} = 22\overline{)568}^{\text{quotient}} = \text{dividend}$$

STEP 1: Guess the largest number of times the divisor 22 fits into 56, the first two digits of the dividend 568. The answer is 2, because:

$$22 \times 2 = 44 < 56 \text{ and } 22 \times 3 = 66 > 56,$$

where < means "less than" and > means "greater than."

The first digit of the quotient is 2.

STEP 2: Multiply the divisor 22 by the quotient 2 that you just found in Step 1. Set 44, the product, under the first two digits 56 of the dividend 568, and subtract 44 from 56, obtaining 12. Lower the next digit 8 of the dividend next to the 12:

$$
\begin{array}{r}
2 \\
22\overline{)568} \\
22 \times 2 = 44 \\
\hline
128.
\end{array}
$$

STEP 3: Guess how many times 22 fits into 128. It is 5, because: $22 \times 5 = 110 < 128$ and $22 \times 6 = 132 > 128$.

The second figure of the quotient is 5. At this step, the quotient is 25 with a **remainder** of 18:

$$
\begin{array}{r}
25 \\
22\overline{)568} \\
44 \\
\hline
128 \\
5 \times 22 = 110 \\
\hline
18.
\end{array}
$$

STEP 4: If a more accurate result is needed, continue the operational steps used above in order to obtain additional figures of the quotient by multiplying the last remainder 18 by 10, obtaining 180; find how many times 22 fits into 180, and repeat the preceding steps as many times as you need additional digits, to get the required accuracy after the dot of the quotient.

$$
\begin{array}{r}
25.81 \\
22\overline{)568.00} \\
44 \\
\hline
128 \\
\end{array}
$$

$5 \times 22 = \quad \underline{110}$

$18 \times 10 = 180$

$8 \times 22 = \underline{176}$

$4 \times 10 = 40$

$1 \times 22 = \underline{22}$

$18.$

The operation of division is the most complicated of the four operations of arithmetic. Currently, it is performed most of the time by means of handheld calculators or electronic computers. But, of course, it is essential to learn how to divide to check the calculator's results, since even the most skilled operator of equipment runs the risk of pushing the wrong key and accepting a wrong result as right. In any case, the result of a division can always be checked by multiplying the obtained quotient by the divisor and comparing the product with the dividend. In our example, the check by multiplication gives:

$$
\begin{array}{r}
25.81 \\
\times \quad 22 \\
\hline
51.62 \\
+516.20 \\
\hline
567.82, \\
\end{array}
$$

a number near enough to the dividend 568 for all practical purposes, indicating that the division steps have been done correctly.

Before solving the problems of Math Camp 6, I wish to introduce you to one more shorthand symbol frequently used in accounting (that is, in dealing with money). The symbol %, which appears on the keyboard of typewriters and computers, is read as "percent" and is used after a number to indicate that it must be divided by 100. For example, 15% is the same as 15/100 (which may be written as 0.15). Therefore, "25% of $1,200" means "multiply (25/100) by $1,200," or $30,000/100 = $300.

1 A car manufacturer builds a car at a cost of $4,550 and sells it to a dealer at a profit of 10%. The dealer sells it to a customer at a profit of 20%. How much does the customer pay for the car?

2 In a car race the third-place winner drove at 100 miles per hour, the second-place winner 10% faster, and the winner 20% faster than the second-place winner. How fast did the winner of the race drive in miles per hour (mph)?

3 The tallest buildings in New York City, the twin towers of the World Trade Center, are each 1,300 feet tall and have 110 floors. What is the average height of a floor of the towers, to the nearest foot?

4 The steps of a staircase in a building are 9 inches tall. How many steps are needed to go from one floor to the next if the floor height in the building is 9 feet?

5 An area of 520,000 square feet in the heart of Chicago is to be subdivided into lots of 200 by 200 feet. How many lots will be obtained?

6 Marathon races are run on a course 26.2 miles long. This year's New York City champion won the race in 2 hours and 10 minutes (2 × 60 + 10 = 130 min.). At what average speed did the champion run in minutes per mile?

7 The flying distance between two cities is 4,500 miles and it takes 8 hours to cover the distance by plane. At what average speed do planes fly between the two cities in miles per hour?

8 Seventy-five employees of a company buy a lotto ticket together and win $22.5 million. How much does each employee win?

9 The area of a building lot in the center of Los Angeles is 900 square feet and sells for $2,115,000. How much does the lot cost per square foot?

10 An ant is 0.125 inches long. You see an ant family move in a line 15 feet long. How many ants are there in the line?

11 Mary buys one pint of vanilla ice cream, one of strawberry, and one of chocolate at the same price for a total of $5.97. How much does the ice cream cost per pint?

12 A wholesaler buys a stock of 397 dresses for $59,550 and sells the dresses at retail for $200 each. How many dollars profit does he make in this transaction?

13 Using the symbol > for "larger than," state which of the two numbers in each of the following problems is greater than the other:

521,245 and 531,245;

618,000,222 and 618,100,223;

422,112 and 422,111.

14 Using the symbol < for "smaller than," state which of the two numbers in each of the following problems is smaller than the other:

234.87 and 243.92;

0.5742 and 0.0963;

123,765,234 and 123,675,234.

15 Jack deposits $100 into his bank account. The interest on the deposit grows 5% every 6 months. How much money does Jack have in the bank 2 years later?

Chapter 3

More Operations on Numbers

🎲 THE NUMBER LINE

When you drive on a highway you often find signs that tell you how far you are from the next town or the next crossroads, like "Albany, 250 miles" or "Route 90, 25 miles," and signs that tell you North or South, East or West. In this way, you learn that you are traveling from New York City toward Washington, D.C. (for example).

On some maps, distances and directions are shown by means of a **number line**, a horizontal or vertical line segment with a dot at midpoint (marked O and called **origin**), on which distances are marked in scale from the origin. The points on the number line are usually (but not always) marked + to the right of or above the origin and – to the left of or below the origin. Fig. 2 is an example of a horizontal number line.

The + numbers to the right of the origin are called **positive**, and the – numbers to the left of the origin, **negative**. A number line

Figure 2 A number line with the origin marked O, positive numbers to the right, and negative numbers to the left.

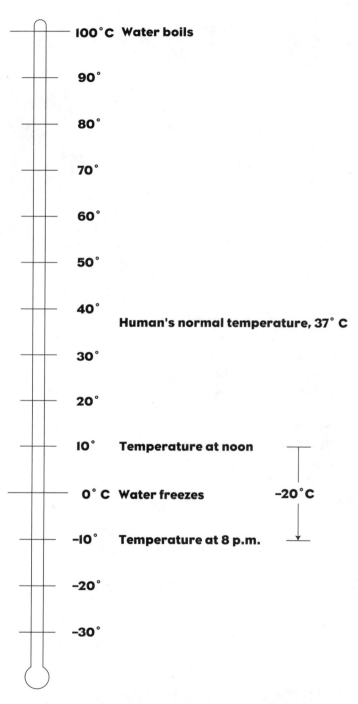

100°C Water boils

90°

80°

70°

60°

50°

40°

Human's normal temperature, 37° C

30°

20°

10° **Temperature at noon**

0° C **Water freezes** **−20°C**

−10° **Temperature at 8 p.m.**

−20°

−30°

Figure 3 Thermometer with temperature scale in degrees centigrade (example of vertical number line).

is a good visual aid in a variety of situations, as shown by the following example of a vertical number line.

Your outdoor thermometer shows a temperature of 10°C (**centigrade**) at noon on a winter day. By 8 p.m. the temperature has gone down by 20°C. (In the centigrade temperature scale, 0°C is the temperature at which water freezes and 100°C is the temperature at which water boils.) What temperature does the thermometer show at 8 p.m.?

The answer to this problem should be obtained by subtracting 20°C from 10°C, but we don't know how to do this yet because we have always subtracted a smaller subtrahend from a larger minuend. To eliminate this difficulty let us agree that, when subtracting a greater subtrahend from a smaller minuend, we will invert these two numbers and perform the subtraction:

$$\begin{array}{r} 20°C \\ -10°C \\ \hline 10°C \end{array}$$

and then put a − (minus) sign in front of the difference. This shows that the temperature at 8 p.m. was −10°C; that is, 10 degrees below zero centigrade.

This example is made visual in Fig. 3, in which the

number line is vertical, with higher temperatures going up. The distance from the point +10°C to the point –10°C shows that the difference between the positive temperature at noon and the negative temperature at 8 p.m. is 20°C.

Thinking about temperatures is a good way to check yourself when writing the symbols > and < ("greater than" and "less than;" see Chapter Two). For example, when you write 10 > 5, ask yourself: "Is 10 degrees higher (warmer) than 5 degrees?" Since you know it is (you can "feel" it), you know you wrote the mathematical statement correctly. Thinking this way makes it easier to write and understand comparisons involving negative numbers. For example, if you want to make sure that –2 < 3 is correct, ask yourself "Is two degrees below zero less (cooler) than three degrees above zero?" Similarly, if you write –10 > –15, you know it is right because 10 degrees below zero is greater (warmer) than 15 degrees below zero.

Math Camp 7

1 You would like to buy a chocolate bar that costs $0.80, but you have only 2 quarters in your pocket. How much do you have to borrow from your friend John to buy the chocolate bar, and how much will you be in debt?

2 You are climbing a mountain when, at a height of 1,300 feet, you suddenly fall 10 feet down. Show your position on a vertical number line with origin at 1,250 feet.

3 You have $200 in your bank account and borrow $500 from the bank. What is your debt to the bank?

4 You live on the ninth floor of an apartment building with 10-foot-high floors. The only elevator in the building is out of order. How many feet do you have to descend to reach your friend on the second floor? Show your descent on a vertical number line with origin on the 10th floor (the top floor) of your building.

5 If you use the symbols > and <, there are two correct ways to write mathematical statements comparing –17 and –29. Write them both. Then write two sentences using degrees on a temperature scale to explain the statements.

⬡ EXPONENTS

You recall how, from the two basic operations of addition and subtraction, mathematicians derived the more efficient shorthand operations of multiplication and division. These operations are capable of solving more difficult problems in an easier fashion.

But shorthand math does not stop there. The French philosopher and mathematician René Descartes, who lived from 1596 to 1650, suggested in a letter to a mathematician friend that rather than writing $2 \times 2 \times \ldots 28$ times, as required by the problem he was solving, he was going to use the shorthand operational symbol "2_{28}." He probably was not immediately aware that, by doing so, he had invented a useful new shorthand notation for the multiplication of identical numbers. Today we write 2^{28} rather than 2_{28}, as suggested by Descartes. This notation is now called exponentiation, as we discussed briefly in Chapter One, Section 6. We call 2 the base and 28 the exponent of the exponential number 2^{28}. Performing the operation 2^{28} is said to **raise 2 to the 28th power**.

Because the area of a square of side length n is equal to $n \times n = n^2$, raising a number to the second power is called **squaring** the number (see Fig. 4).

Similarly, because the volume of a cube of side n is equal to $n \times n \times n = n^3$, raising a number to the third power is called **cubing** the number (see Fig. 5).

Recall from Chapter One that any number n (other than 0) with 0 as the exponent represents the digit 1, or $n^0 = 1$.

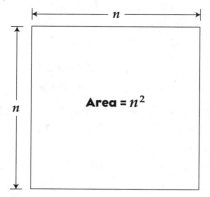

Figure 4 Raising a number to the second power is called **squaring the number** because $n \times n = n^2$ is the area of a square with side lengths equal to n.

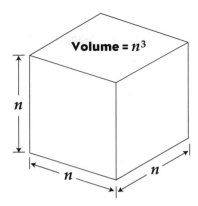

Figure 5 Raising a number to the third power is called **cubing the number** because $n \times n \times n = n^3$ is the volume of a cube with side lengths equal to n.

We use exponential notation with base 10 quite often when we abbreviate the powers of 10 in our decimal system. For example:

$$10^0 = 1 \text{ (one)}$$
$$10^1 = 10 \text{ (ten)}$$
$$10^2 = 100 \text{ (one hundred)}$$
$$10^3 = 1{,}000 \text{ (one thousand)}$$
$$10^4 = 10{,}000 \text{ (ten thousand)}$$
$$10^5 = 100{,}000 \text{ (one hundred thousand)}$$
$$10^6 = 1{,}000{,}000 \text{ (one million)}$$
$$10^9 = 1{,}000{,}000{,}000 \text{ (one billion)}$$
$$10^{12} = 1{,}000{,}000{,}000{,}000 \text{ (one trillion)}$$

If you wonder where such enormous numbers are used, you may want to know that trillions are used in computing the budget of the United States federal government in dollars, and that much, much larger exponential numbers are needed to measure the distances of the stars from the earth. (Such large numbers are used in calculators, where they are written with the exponent separated by some space from the multiplier, rather than above and to the right of the base; for example, 1.23 17 means 1.23×10^{17}.)

You will learn how negative exponents are used as shorthand operational symbols for the operation of division by identical numbers in Section 6 of this chapter.

To solve the following problems involving exponential numbers, you may either patiently multiply or else use a hand calculator with an exponential key that will show the base as x and the exponent as y; that is, the key marked x^y.

1 You were given 2 bunnies, 1 male and 1 female, on your third birthday. To your surprise, within 6 months the female bunny gave birth to 6 new bunnies (3 males and 3 females), so that you found yourself with 8 bunnies (4 males, 4 females). After that, within the following 6 months, each female bunny gave birth to 6 more little bunnies (again, 3 males and 3 females), so that now you have 8 + 4 × 6 = 32 bunnies (again, half males and half females; or 16 males, 16 females). How many new bunnies did you have after 2 years?

You may be amazed to know that if you had kept the bunnies for 4 years you would have found yourself responsible for:

$$2 \times 4 \times 4 \times 4 \times 4 \times 4 \times 4 \times 4 \times 4 = 2 \times 4^8 = 131{,}072 \text{ bunnies!!}$$

You can now appreciate why the fast growth of any quantity is called exponential growth.

2 Your father bought a $10,000 U.S. Treasury Bond the day you were born. This type of bond pays a compounded annual interest of 6%; that is, each year adds 6/100 = 0.06 of the value of the bond to its value at the end of that year. (Another way of saying this is that each year, the amount in the account is multiplied by 1.06.)

Your father gives you the bond the day you become 18 years old, to cover the needs of your college education. How many dollars is he giving you? (Express exponentially the value of your bond at your 18th birthday and compute it in dollars on a calculator or by hand.)

3 John is a chess champion. He bets that Jack cannot beat him. "If you beat me," he says, "I will give you anything you want." Jack answers: "If I beat you, I want you to put 1 cent on a corner square of the chess board, 2 cents on the next, 4 cents on the next, and keep doubling the number of cents you put on each square until you have covered the first three rows of the board."

Jack beat John. Express, in exponential notation, the amount of money John had to give him and compute it in dollars, remembering that a chess board consists of eight rows of eight squares each (Fig. 6).

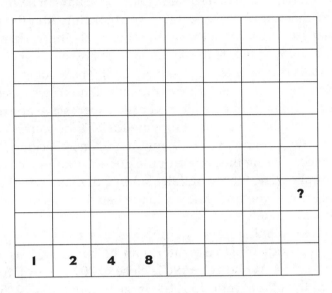

Figure 6 Chessboard with 1 cent on a corner square, 2 cents on the next, 4 cents on the next, and keep doubling the number on each square. How much money is needed to complete 3 rows?

4 The lotus is an aquatic plant with wide leaves growing over an area of 2 square feet. The lotus reproduces very rapidly: in 1 week, three lotuses grow for each lotus planted in the water. How many weeks will it take to cover the entire surface of a pond having an area of 680 square feet with lotuses, if you plant one lotus a week in the pond?

🎲 ROOTS

The garden in the back of your house has a square shape, 10 feet on each side. Its area, the square of the side, is therefore 10 feet × 10 feet = 10^2 square feet = 100 square feet. Because the area of a square is equal to the second power of its side, the second power of a number is called its **square**, and the operation of multiplying a number by itself is called squaring a number.

The garden in the back of your friend John's house is also a square, with an area of 144 square feet. What is the length of the sides of John's garden? Finding the sides of a square, given its area, is the inverse operation to squaring; it is called **extracting the square root**, and its operational symbol is $\sqrt{}$. For John's garden, each side is easily found to be 12 feet, since from a multiplication table (Table 4 in Chapter Two) we see that $12^2 = 144$.

But often the area of a square is not the square of a whole number. A mathematical process, called an **algorithm** after the great Persian mathematician of the ninth century, al-Khowarizmi, has been devised to evaluate the square root of any number (which, of course, does not have to represent an area). The trouble is that the square-root algorithm is rather complicated. It is often easier to evaluate a square root by a method called **successive approximations**. This method consists of moving toward the square root by successively guessing its value, squaring it, and checking the result by comparing the square of the guess with the value of the given number. The following calculation will make this simple and most useful method (known to the Babylonians in 2,000 B.C.) easily understood.

Let's assume that John's garden has an area of 200 square feet. Then its side must be greater than 12, because 12^2 is only 144. Let's try 14. While $14^2 = 196$ is close to 200, it is still too small. On the other hand, 15 is too large because $15^2 = 225$ is much larger than 200. Let's now try a number closer to 14 than 15, say, 14.2. Squaring this gives $14.2^2 = 201.64$, still too large but not by much, while $14.1^2 = 198.81$ is too small. Trying a number larger than 14.1 and smaller than 14.2, say $14.15^2 = 200.22$, we find a number that is an acceptable approximation of the true value of the square root of 200. (For your own information and to satisfy your curiosity, the square root of 200, evaluated by electronic calculator, is 14.14213562. Our last approximation, 14.15, is wrong by only one unit in the fourth digit.)

Because the volume of a cube (Fig. 5) is equal to the third power of its side (as you know from Section 2 of this chapter), the third power of a number is called its **cube**. Finding the length of the side of a cube, given its volume, or finding the cube root of any given number, is called **extracting the cube root** of the number and symbolized by the operational symbol $\sqrt[3]{}$. Similarly, all the roots above the square root are symbolized by $\sqrt{}$ with the order of the root in front of the root symbol, such as $\sqrt[4]{}$ for the fourth root. (The order 2 of the square root is done away with, because the square root is so commonly met that it is simply called "the root.")

Roots of higher order are usually evaluated by successive approximations, although the availability of hand calculators and computers allows immediate answers. It may be obvious, but useful, to notice that roots of certain powers of 2 may be computed by repeatedly evaluating square roots. For example, the fourth root of a number may be computed as the square root of the square root of the number, since 2 is the square root of 4:

$$\sqrt[4]{16} = \sqrt{\sqrt{16}} = \sqrt{4} = 2;$$
$$\sqrt[8]{256} = \sqrt{\sqrt{\sqrt{256}}} = \sqrt{\sqrt{16}} = \sqrt{4} = 2.$$

The same procedure can be used for roots that are powers of some other whole number, by taking repeated roots of the order of that number. For example,

$$\sqrt[9]{512} = \sqrt[3]{\sqrt[3]{512}} = \sqrt[3]{8} = 2.$$

I suggest that in solving the following problems in Math Camp 9, which require the evaluation of roots, you use the method of successive approximations, because it is an extremely useful procedure for solving many interesting problems besides those involving roots.

Math Camp 9

1 The main square of a town with four equal sides has an area of 4 acres. What is the length of its sides in feet? (An acre is equal to 43,560 square feet.)

2 A cubic wooden crate must have a volume of 1,000 cubic feet. What is the length of its sides in feet?

3 A die has a volume of 0.125 cubic inches. What is the length of its sides in inches?

4 The business district of a town has a rectangular shape with one pair of opposite sides twice the length of the other pair of opposite sides (Fig. 7). The area of the rectangle is 30,000 square feet. What are the lengths of the long and the short sides of the rectangle?

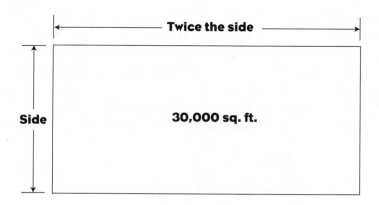

Figure 7 Math Camp 9, problem 4.

⬛ FRACTIONS

We noticed in Section 4 of Chapter Two that among the various symbols used to represent the operation of division, a common one is a horizontal bar with the dividend above it and the divisor below it as, for example:

$$\frac{24}{12}$$

and

$$\frac{15,209.7}{41.7}$$

The same symbol is used to represent the **ratio** of two numbers, particularly when the numbers measure physical quantities like length, volume, temperature, or force. Let us use the concept of ratio in a simple example.

For her birthday Mary received a round cake from her parents, and she shared it with her brother, her mother, and her father by dividing it into four equal parts (Fig. 8). Each member of the family got one-fourth of the cake, in a ratio of 1 to 4 of the whole cake. This ratio is represented by the symbol 1/4 and is called a **fraction.** When referring to a fraction, the upper number, or dividend, of the division is called the **numerator** and the lower number, or divisor, is called the **denominator.**

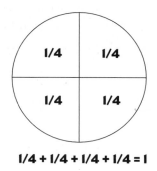

1/4 + 1/4 + 1/4 + 1/4 = 1

Figure 8 A cake cut into four equal parts. The sum of the parts equals one whole cake.

All fractions may be translated into decimal form by dividing the upper number by the lower number:

$$\frac{1}{2} = 0.5;$$

$$\frac{1}{3} = 0.33333\ldots;$$

$$\frac{15,207.7}{42.7} = 356.2,$$

but a fraction may also be considered a numerical entity in itself. The operations of arithmetic may be applied to fractions without first performing the division and converting the fraction to decimal form. Let us find out how to perform the four operations of arithmetic on fractions.

🎲 OPERATIONS ON FRACTIONS

Mary's family divided her birthday cake into four equal parts and she ate one-fourth of it. How much cake did each of the other three members of the family eat?

Assuming that each ate the same amount of cake, the remaining three of them ate:

$$1/4 + 1/4 + 1/4 = 3/4$$

of the cake. We have been able to obtain this result by simply adding the numerators of the three fractions because they all had the same denominator; that is, each of the four family members had eaten the same amount of cake.

Let us now assume that Mary's brother ate half, that is, 1/2, of the cake and the three other family members ate three equal parts of the remaining cake (Fig. 9). How much of the cake did Mary and her brother eat?

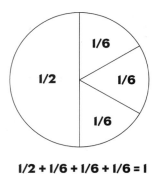

1/2 + 1/6 + 1/6 + 1/6 = 1

Figure 9 A cake cut into two halves, with one of those halves cut into three equal parts. The sum of the parts equals one whole cake. See Figure 10.

This time, because their denominators are different, we cannot just add the numerators of the two fractions. We can only add the numerators after making their denominators equal. This is simple because one can always multiply the numerator and the denominator of a fraction by the same number without changing the value of the fraction. Since a fraction represents the division of two numbers, it is obvious that multiplying (or dividing) dividend and divisor by the same number does not change the value of the quotient. For example, look at the fraction 3/5:

$$3/5 = 0.6, \text{ and } (3 \times 2)/(5 \times 2) = 6/10 = 0.6.$$

The operation of giving different fractions the same denominator, thus without changing their value, is called finding a **common denominator** of the fractions. As an example of the simplest way to find a common denominator, let us consider the case of Mary's brother eating one-half of the cake and Mary eating one-third of the remaining cake. As shown in Fig. 10, Mary eats one-sixth of the cake, proving that the product of two fractions is equal to the product of their two numerators divided by the product of their two denominators:

$$1/3 \times 1/2 = (1 \times 1)/(3 \times 2) = 1/6.$$

Let us now add the 1/2 cake eaten by Mary's brother to the 1/6 cake eaten by Mary, taking as the common denominator the

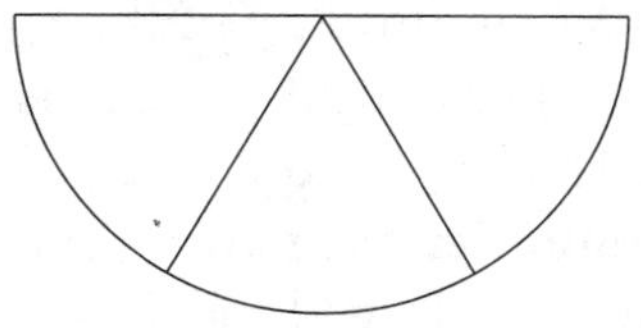

(Half of a cake)

1/3 x 1/2 = (1 x 1)/(3 x 2) = 1/6

Figure 10 One-third of one-half (of a cake) equals one-sixth (of a cake). See Figure 9.

product of the two denominators 2 and 6; that is, 12. In order not to change the values of the two fractions, we first multiply the numerator and denominator of the first fraction, 1/2, by the denominator, 6, of the second fraction. We also multiply the numerator and denominator of the second fraction by the denominator, 2, of the first fraction. Once the two fractions have a common denominator, we add their numerators, then simplify.

$$1/2 + 1/6 = (1 \times 6)/(2 \times 6) + (1 \times 2)/(6 \times 2)$$
$$= 6/12 + 2/12 = (6 + 2)/12 = 8/12 = 2/3.$$

Mary and her brother together ate 2/3 of the cake, so if each parent ate half of the 1/3 remaining cake, each ate only 1/6 of the cake (not fair for the people who paid for the cake, but being parents, they probably don't mind).

So far, we have learned how to add and multiply fractions. Now let's find out how to subtract and divide them.

Subtraction results from getting a common denominator for the fractions and then subtracting the numerators, as in the following example:

$$3/5 - 1/4 = (3 \times 4)/(5 \times 4) - (1 \times 5)/(4 \times 5)$$
$$= 12/20 - 5/20 = (12 - 5)/20 = 7/20.$$

It may be useful to give a suggestion that simplifies the evaluation of common denominators. Let us add the three fractions:

$$3/2 + 4/5 + 3/10,$$

and notice that since $10 = 2 \times 5$ is the common denominator of the first two fractions, it is simpler to use 10 as the common denominator for all these fractions, rather than $2 \times 5 \times 10 = 100$:

$$(5 \times 3)/(5 \times 2) + (2 \times 4)/(2 \times 5) + 3/10 = 15/10$$
$$+ 8/10 + 3/10 = 26/10 = 13/5.$$

In other words, to find a common denominator of many fractions, it is simpler to use the product of the terms common to as many fractions as possible multiplied by the factors uncommon to the other fractions. This procedure leads to the idea of the smallest or **least common denominator**. (In the previous example, the final result, 26/10, allowed the division of the numerator and denominator by 2 only because, by mere chance, both these numbers were even.)

To divide one fraction by another fraction, all we have to remember is that a fraction does not change value if we multiply the numerator and denominator by the same number. (In this example, we will use both the symbol / and the symbol —— to indicate division, in order to make clear its various steps.)

To perform the division:

$$\frac{(2/5)}{(3/7),} \tag{a}$$

we start by multiplying the numerator and the denominator of the fraction (a) by the denominator 7 of 3/7, thus not changing the value of (a):

$$\frac{(2/5)}{(3/7)} = \frac{(2/5) \times 7}{(3/7) \times 7} = \frac{(2/5) \times 7}{3 \times (7/7).} \tag{b}$$

Since $7/7 = 1$, we obtain the fraction:

$$\frac{(2/5) \times 7}{3.} \tag{c}$$

We now divide the numerator and denominator of (c) by 3:

$$\frac{(2/5) \times (7/3)}{3/3} = (2/5) \times (7/3) = \frac{2 \times 7}{5 \times 3} = \frac{14}{15.} \tag{d}$$

The final result of this sequence of operations shows that to divide 2/5 by 3/7, all one has to do is multiply the numerator fraction 2/5 of (a) by the inverse of the denominator fraction 3/7 of (a); that is, multiply 2/5 by 7/3, the inverse of 3/7. (In many books this result is given as a rule: "To divide two fractions, multiply the first by the inverse of the second." I prefer to show you where this "rule" comes from, because I believe that math operations should be understood rather than accepted, since there are no rules, ever, in mathematics.)

If one has to multiply a fraction by a whole number, all one has to do is to multiply the numerator by the number, since the

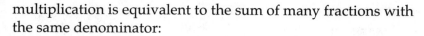

multiplication is equivalent to the sum of many fractions with the same denominator:

$$3 \times (2/5) = 2/5 + 2/5 + 2/5 = (2 + 2 + 2)/5 = (3 \times 2)/5 = 6/5.$$

If one must divide a fraction by a whole number, one may write the number as a fraction with the denominator equal to 1 and apply the above-mentioned "rule":

$$(6/13)/2 = (6/13)/(2/1) = (6/13) \times (1/2)$$
$$= (6 \times 1)/(13 \times 2) = 6/26 = 3/13,$$

or, more simply, divide the numerator of the fraction by the whole number, since the denominator 1 has no influence on the result:

$$(6/13)/2 = (6/2)/13 = 3/13.$$

The powers (or the roots) of a fraction are evaluated by dividing the powers (or the roots) of the numerator by the powers (or the roots) of the denominator, since powers are shorthand symbols of successive multiplications (or divisions):

$$(2/5)^3 = 2^3/5^3 = 8/125.$$

$$\sqrt{4/16} = \sqrt{4}/\sqrt{16} = 2/4 = 1/2.$$

——— Math  Camp ———
10

1 Mount Everest (called Cholomongma in Nepalese), the highest mountain on earth, is 29,300 feet high; Mount McKinley in Alaska, the highest mountain in the United States, is 20,320 feet high. What is the ratio of the height of Mount McKinley to that of Mount Everest?

2 John saves $75 and Mary $50 at Christmas. What is the ratio of Mary's to John's savings as a fraction?

3 John receives 3/5 and Mary 1/3 of a gift of $125 from their parents. What is the ratio of Mary's to John's gift, as a fraction? How much is the sum of the two gifts, in dollars?

4 Jules receives a gift of money from his mother and gives 1/5 of it to his brother and 1/5 of it to his sister. What ratio of the gift is Jules left with, as a fraction of his mother's gift?

5 Mr. Gold has a yearly income of $100,000 and gives 10% of it to charities. He gives 3/5 of his charity to the Single Hospital, 1/4 to the Boy Scouts, and the rest to a homeless woman. How much do the hospital, the Boy Scouts, and the homeless woman get in dollars?

6 George gets a $90 Christmas gift from his grandmother and gives 1/3 of it to his sister and 1/4 of it to his brother. How much money is George left with, in dollars and as a fraction of his grandmother's gift?

7 The minority population of an American town consists of 1/3 African Americans, 1/4 Koreans, 1/5 Chinese, and 1/6 Arabs. What is the ratio of all the minority populations to the entire population of the town, as a fraction? As a percentage?

8 You had $90 in your savings account on December 31 of last year. You spent 1/5 of it in January, 1/8 of it in February, and 1/6 of it in March. On April 30, you put $30 into the account. What fraction of the money you had on December 31 do you have in the account on April 30?

9 The winner of a car race covers the 500 miles of the circuit in 3 hours, the second-place winner in 3 hours and 15 minutes, and the third-place winner in 3 hours and 20 minutes. What are the ratios of the speeds of the second- and third-place winners to that of the first, and of that of the third-place winner to that of the second? Translate the times of the three winners into minutes and express the speeds as fractions, in units of miles per minute (mi./min.).

10 You bought meat during 4 different weeks: 1/2 pound the first, 4/5 pound the second, 1 1/3 pounds the third, and 2 pounds the fourth. How many pounds did you buy in those 4 weeks? (Express the result as a fraction of a pound.)

11 You are choosing which one of four cars to buy. The first sells for $18,000 at no discount, the second for $20,000 at 12% discount, the third for $21,000 at 15% discount, and the fourth at $19,000 at 7% discount. Which is the cheapest and which the most expensive of the four cars?

12 A square building lot has an area of 45,000 acres; a second square building lot has an area of 60,000 acres. What is the ratio of the area of the first lot to the area of the second lot? Compute the answer both as a fraction and as a decimal number.

13 What is the ratio of the sides of a 27-cubic-foot cubic container to those of a 64-cubic-foot cubic container?

⚅ WORKING WITH NEGATIVE NUMBERS

We learned in Section 1 of this chapter that in arithmetic the symbols + and – have two different meanings: a **positional** value on the number line, and an **operational** value in the operations of addition and subtraction. (We also learned that the temperature scale, with degrees above and below zero, is a useful way to think about these ideas.) We found that in the operation of subtraction, when the number to be subtracted (the subtrahend) is larger than the number it is subtracted from (the minuend), the result of the operation (the difference) is a new type of number we call negative and label with a minus sign:

$$(+15) - (+23) = 15 - 23 = -8.$$

The minus sign between 15 and 23 is operational, while the minus sign in front of the difference, –8, is positional, indicating that –8 is located on the number line eight units to the left of the origin (–8° on a thermometer).

We must now investigate how to perform the four operations of arithmetic with both positive and negative numbers. In what follows, we will temporarily indicate the positional values of + and – in front of the numbers inside the parentheses, and their operational values in front of the parenthesis. (Later on we shall drop the + positional signs in front of positive numbers, and retain only the – sign in front of negative numbers, as is done in mathematical practice.)

The following four examples of addition and subtraction illustrate the "rules" to be used with positive and negative numbers (remember to think about temperatures above and below zero):

$$(+10) + (+2) = (+12) = 12;$$
$$(-10) + (-5) = (-15) = -15;$$
$$(+10) - (+2) = (+8) = 8;$$
$$(+8) - (+10) = (-2) = -2.$$

The first two examples show that in the operation of addition, the combination of operational and positional values results in the following two "rules":

$$(+) + (+) = (+) = +;$$
$$(-) + (-) = (-) = -.$$

In the operation of subtraction, the last two examples show that:

(+) – (+) = (+) = + if the first number is greater than the second;
(+) – (+) = (–) = – if the second number is greater than the first.

Of course, we always get zero when we subtract two identical numbers, whether they are positive such as (+8) – (+8) = 0, or negative such as (–8) – (–8) = 0. We also get zero when we add a positive number to its negative, such as (+8) + (–8) = 0. If we look at the first and third of these examples, we see that

(+8) – (+8) = (+8) + (–8),

which, in words, means that subtracting a positive number gives the same result as adding the negative of that number. That is, – (+) = + (–), where the same number appears inside the parentheses after the plus and minus signs. This is always true, but it may take some work to understand.

Actually, it took many centuries for people to invent the concept of negative numbers. Many bright people refused to accept them because they had trouble understanding how to use them. In fact, one could almost imagine that we call them "negative" numbers because so many people had negative feelings about them!

The number line (or temperature scale) is a good way to understand addition of positive and negative numbers. For example, Fig. 11 shows

(+3) + (–7) = (–4) = –4,

which, we now know, is the same as (+3) – (+7) = –4.

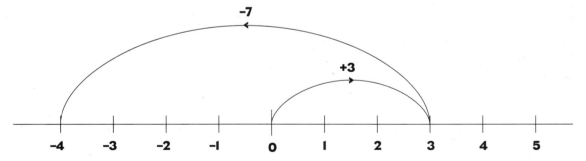

Figure 11 Using the number line to show addition of positive and negative numbers. The example shows (+3) + (–7) = –4, which is the same as (+3) – (+7) = –4.

Since the operation of multiplication is a shorthand for the operation of addition, the corresponding rules, with examples, are:

a) $(+) \times (+) = (+) = +;$ $2 \times 3 = 6;$
b) $(+) \times (-) = (-) = -;$ $2 \times (-3) = (-6) = -6;$
c) $(-) \times (+) = (-) = -;$ $(-3) \times 2 = -6;$
d) $(-) \times (-) = (+) = +;$ $(-3) \times (-2) = (+6) = 6.$

The four rules for the operation of multiplication may be easily remembered by setting "road signs" + and – on the number line and attributing to the road signs the following meanings:

+ means: keep going in the same direction in which you are going;
  – means: turn around and go in the opposite direction.

Thus the four examples a), b), c), d) can be described as follows by remembering the meaning of the road signs:

a) If you are moving in the + direction and meet a + road sign, keep going in the + direction;
b) If you are moving in the + direction and meet a – road sign, turn around and move in the – direction;
c) If you are moving in the – direction and meet a + road sign, keep going in the – direction;
d) If you are moving in the – direction and meet a – road sign, turn around and move in the + direction.

The same four "rules" apply to the operation of division, a shorthand for the operation of subtraction, as shown in the following examples:

$$24/8 \quad = +3;$$
$$24/(-8) = -3;$$
$$-24/8 \quad = -3;$$
$$-24/(-8) = +3.$$

Since we have been introduced to the operation of exponentiation as a shorthand for the operation of multiplication, we must finally learn the meaning of the + and – symbols in the exponent. This is particularly important because the meaning of the – sign in the exponent is to invert the operations of multiplication and division, as shown below in examples 3) and 4):

1) $2^3 = (+2) \times (+2) \times (+2) = 8;$
2) $(-2)^3 = (-2) \times (-2) \times (-2) = (+4) \times (-2) = -8;$
3) $2^{-3} = 1/2 \times 1/2 \times 1/2 = 1/2^3 = 1/8;$
4) $(-2)^{-3} = 1/(-2) \times 1/(-2) \times 1/(-2) = 1/4 \times 1/(-2) = 1/(-8) = -1/8.$

The examples show that a negative exponent means inversion of the same exponentiation with a positive exponent:

$$3^{-2} = 1/(3^2) = 1/9;$$
$$2^{-3} = 1/(2^3) = 1/8;$$
$$(-4)^{-2} = 1/(-4)^2 = 1/16.$$

Whenever possible, express the operations in exponential form before solving the following problems.

1   You have a savings account in which you deposit and from which you withdraw money. Let us agree to call + a deposit and – a withdrawal, and measure forward time as + and backward time as –.

   a) You had $100 in your account and you deposited $20 in it every week for 4 weeks. How much richer did you become? [(+) + (+)] = +.

   b) You had $130 in the account and you withdrew $15 a week for 4 weeks. How much poorer did you become? [(–) + (–)] = –.

   c) You had $100 in the account and you deposited $20 in it every week for 3 weeks. How much poorer were you 3 weeks ago than you are now? [(+) x (–)] = –.

   d) You had $200 in the account and you withdrew $25 a week for 4 weeks. How much richer were you 4 weeks ago than you are now? [(–) x (–)] = +.

2   You loaned $10 a week to a friend for 3 weeks. He returned $25 in a lump sum after 3 weeks. How many dollars did you lose?

3   Three weeks ago, the temperature was 10 degrees Fahrenheit = +10°F. Your outdoor thermometer shows the temperature went down 5°F each day since then. What is the centigrade temperature today? (See the relationship between °F and °C in Chapter Four, Section 1.)

4   Your outdoor thermometer showed a temperature of –10°C a week ago. The temperature has gone up 3°C per day since then. What was the temperature two days ago in degrees centigrade?

5 You buy a bushel of apples containing 45 apples for $15. Upon getting home you find that 10 apples are rotten. How much money did you waste? How much did each good apple cost?

6 The temperature in New York City last winter went down from 20°C to –10°C in a week. How many degrees centigrade did the temperature go down per day, on average?

7 Last Monday the stock of Company A was worth $150. This Monday it is quoted at $110. On average, how much did the stock value of Company A change per day?

8 Mount Everest, the highest mountain on earth, is 29,300 feet high. The deepest point at the bottom of the Indian Ocean is 33,300 feet under sea level. What is the vertical distance between the top of Mount Everest and the bottom of the Indian Ocean?

9 A store bought 1,000 pairs of shoes at $30 a pair and sold 750 pairs at $50 a pair. The remaining pairs were sold on sale for $25 a pair. On average, how many dollars did the store make, or lose, for each pair of shoes it sold?

10 John has $1,000 in his bank account at 5% annual interest. He is allowed to borrow up to $2,000 at 10% annual interest. If he borrows $750 for 2 years, how much does he have in his account after returning the amount he borrowed?

11 Express the following numbers exponentially in powers of 10:

1,724,265;   245.572;   0.00275;
0.000000022;   0.000000000003.

12 Express the following exponential numbers in decimal form:

2.75×10^4; 6.125×10^6; 200.25×10^5; 2.3×10^{-2};
1.45×10^{-3}; -4.5×10^{-2}.

13 Today, your bank account has $200 in it and grows 5% a year. What is your balance 10 years from today, if you do not withdraw any money from your account? Express the answer exponentially and then evaluate it in decimal form.

14 The earth was born 4.5×10^9 years ago. Express the age of the earth in decimal form and in words.

15 Today it is believed that the universe was born, in a tremendous explosion called the Big Bang, about 15 billion years ago. Express the age of the universe decimally and exponentially.

16 Express exponentially the number of seconds in 2 hours. Express exponentially 1 second in 1-hour units (1 hr. = 60 × 60 = 3,600 sec.)

17 How many days ago was the universe born, assuming that it was born 14 billion years ago? Express its age exponentially in units of 1 day, assuming a year to be, on average, 365 days long.

18 How many hours ago was the earth born, if it was born 4.5 billion years ago? Express its age exponentially in units of 1 hour.

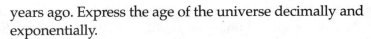 **ESTIMATING AND ROUNDING OFF**

On many occasions it is useful to guess approximately, or **estimate,** a distance, a weight, or a height (or any other physical magnitude), before measuring it exactly. For example, before buying a rug for your bedroom, you might estimate that a rug measuring 3 feet by 5 feet would fit your room. If you find, in a store, a 2.5-foot by 4.5-foot rug that you particularly like, you might buy it even if it is not exactly the size you wanted, because you already know that it will fit your room with a few inches of floor showing around the edge.

Getting good at estimating is extremely useful in everyday life, and you should get into the habit of estimating distances, lengths, amounts of money, lengths of time, and many other physical quantities. I suggest that you estimate some of the following quantities and then actually measure them, whenever possible.

- The heights of your friends and family members.
- The weights of your friends and family members.
- The length and width of each room of your apartment.
- The height of your building, knowing that floors are usually 8 to 10 feet high.
- The number of steps between floors in your building.
- The width and height of the windows of your building.
- The length of a street block, which is usually between 200 and 300 feet.
- The distance between two points in your city based on the length of the blocks one has to walk to get from one to the other.

- How many minutes it will take to walk around the block your building is on, knowing that you walk at a rate of about 2 to 3 miles per hour (mph).
- The length of your family car.
- How many hours it will take to drive from your town to another you'd like to visit, knowing that people drive at about 50 to 60 mph.
- How long it will take to fly from New York to San Francisco, a distance of 3,000 miles, knowing that planes fly at an average speed of 500 mph.
- How far a good batter can hit a baseball, knowing that the diamond of a baseball field is a square measuring 90 feet on each side.
- How many hours and minutes it will take the winner to run a marathon, knowing that a marathon is about 26 miles long, and that the winner runs at an average speed of 12 mph.

I am sure you can find many more quantities to estimate and you might like to compete with your friends to see who gets the best estimates. To judge the competition, you will need to measure the quantities you have estimated.

A particular type of estimating, called **rounding off,** consists of substituting zeros for the lower digits of a number, up to the nearest ten, hundred, thousand, and so on, and then increasing by 1 the first nonzero digit if the last zeroed digit was 5 or greater, and not increasing the first nonzero digit if the last zeroed digit was less than 5. For example, you want to buy cakes for a large party of 237 friends; on the one hand, you do not know for sure if they will all come; on the other hand, you realize that some of your friends may bring along a companion, a spouse, or even a child or two. So you may decide to round off the number of invitees to 240, or, to play it safer, to 250.

Bankers dealing with large sums of money often round off their figures, by ignoring the pennies in comparison with the dollars or the dollar figures in a sum of millions of dollars. For example, after adding the following amounts:

$$
\begin{array}{r}
\$2{,}453{,}617 \\
1{,}602{,}100 \\
642{,}212 \\
\underline{456{,}672} \\
\$5{,}154{,}601,
\end{array}
$$

they may round off the sum to 5 million dollars. As a matter of fact, they would probably have mentally rounded off the sum of the first two numbers to be 4 million, and the last two to 1 million, getting 5 million before carefully summing the four amounts.

Practice rounding off the numbers in the following Math Camp.

12

1 Round off the following numbers to the nearest hundred: 576; 9,460; 10,097; 110,452; 1,000,890; 2,445,667,224.

2 Round off the following numbers to the nearest hundred thousand:

1,095,022; 10,897,252.22; 2,999,754; 1,002,003,004.

3 Your middle school has the following number of students in each class:

Sixth grade, class A: 32 students; class B: 30; class C: 34; class D: 31.

Seventh grade, class A: 33; class B: 32; class C: 30; class D: 34; class E: 32;

Eighth grade, class A: 35; class B: 39; class C: 25.

Round off the number of students in your school to the nearest hundred.

4 In 1980, the populations of the easternmost states of the United States were:

Connecticut	3,107,576
Maine	1,124,860
Massachusetts	5,737,037
New Hampshire	920,610
Rhode Island	947,154
Vermont	511,456

Add these population figures and round off the total to the nearest million.

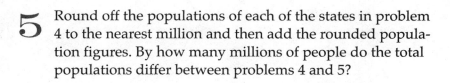

5 Round off the populations of each of the states in problem 4 to the nearest million and then add the rounded population figures. By how many millions of people do the total populations differ between problems 4 and 5?

Chapter 4

Measurements

 WHAT IS MEASURING?

Measuring consists of choosing a **unit** and finding out how many times the unit fits into the quantity we want to measure. For example, we have many units to measure time, and depending on how much time we have to measure, we choose among units such as seconds (sec.), minutes (min.), hours (hr.), days, weeks, months, years, decades, or centuries. Abbreviations such as those in the parentheses above are often used in technical writing.

Temperature is measured in units called degrees. We may use units of degrees Fahrenheit (°F) or degrees centigrade (°C). If F is the temperature in °F, and C is the corresponding temperature in °C, then C and F are related by the equation:

$$F = 9C/5 + 32°F \quad \text{or} \quad C = 5/9 \, (F - 32°F).$$

As you already know, water boils at $F = 212°F$, which is actually the same temperature as $C = 100°C$. Also, water freezes at 32°F = 0°C. Temperatures below 0° (whether Fahrenheit or centigrade) are indicated by putting a minus sign in front of the number, such as –10°F. The two scales happen to have the same value at –40°, as shown in Fig. 12. In symbols, you may write –40°F = –40°C. You should check these facts by substituting various temperatures into the two formulas above.

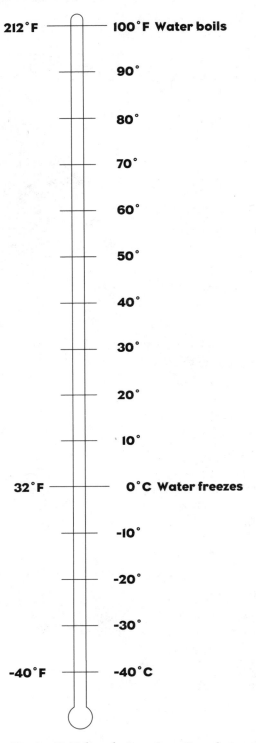

212°F — 100°F Water boils

90°

80°

70°

60°

50°

40°

30°

20°

10°

32°F — 0°C Water freezes

-10°

-20°

-30°

-40°F — -40°C

Figure 12 Fahrenheit and centigrade temperature scales happen to have the same value at –40°.

To measure distance, we may choose units from the **British measurement system.** This is the system that is most familiar to Americans, where a short length is measured in inches (in.), a medium length in feet (ft.) or yards (yd.), and a long length in miles (mi.), remembering that a foot is 12 inches long, a yard is 3 feet long, and a mile is 5,280 feet long.

In the British measurement system, an **area** may be measured in square inches (sq. in.), square feet (sq. ft.), square yards (sq. yd.), or square miles (sq. mi.), and a **volume** in cubic inches (cu. in.), cubic feet (cu. ft.), cubic yards (cu. yd.), or cubic miles (cu. mi.). **Force** is measured in units of weight, such as pounds (lb.) or tons (tn.). (One ton = 2,000 pounds.)

It would be impossible to list all the units needed to measure every quantity we encounter in practice (there are manuals for this purpose). The exercises in Math Camp 13, however, will help to familiarize you with the British units most frequently encountered in daily life.

1 Measure the length of your arm from your shoulder to the tip of your fingers with a tape measure. Express its length in inches (in.) and feet (ft.).

2 Measure the front of your house (or building) in steps and transform it into feet by measuring the length of your average step.

3 A building has 50 floors, each 9 feet high. How high is the building in feet and in yards?

4 The plaza of a town is a rectangle 100 ft. by 150 ft. What is the area of the plaza in sq. ft. and in sq. yd.?

5 A cube has sides 0.63 ft. long. What is the volume of the cube in cubic inches (cu. in.) and in cubic feet (cu. ft.)?

6 The temperature in New York today is 85°F. What is the temperature in °C?

7 Water boils at 100°C and freezes at 0°C. Compute the temperatures in °F at which water boils and freezes.

8 A runner wins a marathon of 26.2 mi. in 2 hr. and 12 min. At what average speed does he run in miles per hour (mph) and in feet per second (ft./sec.)?

9 A plane flies from New York to San Francisco, an air distance of 3,000 mi., in 4 1/2 hr. At what average speed does it fly in mi./hr. and in ft./sec.?

10 A circular water pipe is 100 ft. long and has a diameter of 2 ft. Water flows through the pipe at 1 ft./sec. How much water flows through the pipe in a day, measured in cu. ft?

11 The temperature in Boston was 50°F at 8 a.m. and 20°F at 8 p.m. What are these two temperatures in °C? What was the rate with which the temperature changed from 8 a.m. to 8 p.m. in °C/hr. and in °F/hr.?

12 A cup of coffee reaches your table at the beginning of your meal at a temperature of 90°C. By the end of the meal a half hour later, it is 40°C. At what rate did the coffee become colder during your meal? (Calculate the answer using °F/min.).

13 Concrete that is ready to be poured costs $300 per cu. yd. How much will it cost to fill a trench 100 ft. long, 3 ft. wide, and 4 ft. deep with concrete?

14 The Kelvin temperature scale is identical to the centigrade scale, except for its origin, the so-called absolute zero ($-273°C$), at which atomic particles stop moving. Determine the Kelvin temperatures at which water freezes and at which it boils.

15 How long is 10^3 seconds in minutes? How long is 10^6 hours in centuries?

THE SI SYSTEM

In 1960, almost all the nations of the world agreed to abandon their traditional units of measurement, including the British units, in favor of **SI units,** which are easier to use because the **SI system** is based on the decimal system (powers of 10). "SI" is an abbreviation for "Système international," French for "International System." It is a modification of the "**metric system** of measurements and weights" that was planned in France during the reign of Napoleon (1769–1821) and adopted into French law in 1799. The metric system is based on the unit of length called the **meter,** which was originally supposed to equal 1/40,000 of the earth's circumference. Since the earth is not a perfect sphere, it was later decided to define the meter legally as the length of a bar of a specific metal, called platinum, kept at a rigorously constant temperature in the Science Museum of Paris.

The conquests of Napoleon in Europe and the practicality of the metric system gradually led to its adoption over almost all the world except for the United States and Britain. (George Washington was in favor of the metric system but failed to get it accepted as a law.) In the United States, the SI system was chosen as the preferred system of measurement by the federal government in 1975: at present, any project for the U.S. government must be presented in SI units. The SI system is often referred to as "the modern metric system" in the United States, and the translation from the British system to the SI system of units is referred to as **metrication.**

In the SI system there are no strange **conversion factors,** as in the British system, where, for example, one foot equals 12 inches and one mile equals 5,280 feet. One unit of measure is specified for each physical quantity, and fractions of that unit are measured in powers of 10. For example, the basic unit of length is the meter, and prefixes are used to indicate other lengths. Thus, the **decimeter** is 1/10 of a meter, the **centimeter** is 1/100 of a meter, and the **millimeter** is 1/1 000 of a meter. Longer lengths are measured in decimal multiples of the meter. Thus, the **dekameter** equals 10 meters, and the **kilometer** equals 1 000 meters.

The unit of area is the **square meter** (m^2), which is the area of a square with sides one meter long. The unit of volume is the **cubic meter** (m^3) for solid materials. For liquids, you may use the **liter** (l), which equals a cubic decimeter (which equals 1/1 000 of a cubic meter).

Instead of abbreviations, each unit has a unique **unit symbol** such as *m* for meter or *s* for second. Notice that a unit symbol is not followed by a period. It would take too much space to list all the units of the SI system here, but you should become familiar with the following four. The symbol for each unit is shown in parentheses.

> The unit of length is the meter (m);
> The unit of time is the second (s);
> The unit of **mass** is the kilogram (**kg**);
> The unit of **force** is the **newton** (**N**).

Some units, like the newton, are called "derived" units, meaning they are actually a combination of more basic units, like length, time, and mass.

The word **mass** means an amount of matter, independent of gravity. It should not be confused with the word "weight," which normally means the force with which a mass is attracted by our planet Earth. Your body has the same mass whether you are on the earth, the moon, or elsewhere. However, if you were on the moon, your body would feel like it weighs less than it does on the earth because the pull of gravity on the earth's surface is about six times the pull of gravity on the moon's surface. An object that weighs 1 kg on the earth has the same mass wherever it is. It weighs 2.2 pounds on the earth, but this would only feel like 2.2/6 = 0.37 pounds on the moon. (Knowing your weight in pounds, you should now find it simple to calculate your weight on the moon and your mass in kg.)

Some examples of prefixes used to indicate multiples of units are:

kilo (k) $= 10^3$;
milli (m) $= 1/10^3$;
mega (M) $= 10^6$;
micro (µ) $= 10^{-6}$.

Thus, 27 MN means 27 meganewtons or 27 000 000 newtons.

Notice that in the SI system we use spaces instead of commas to separate every three digits, as in "27 000 000 newtons" above. We also use a comma instead of the decimal dot, as in 2 075 032,345 227 instead of 2,075,032.345227, or 2,75 m instead of 2.75 m.

Three more writing rules for the SI system are:

- Use decimal numbers rather than fractions: 0,75 instead of 3/4.
- Do not use plurals with units: 30 N instead of 30 Ns.
- Leave one space between numbers and units: 24 N instead of 24N.

🎲 HOW TO GET USED TO THE SI SYSTEM

During this transition period from the old British system to the SI system, we all have difficulty in grasping the physical meaning of the quantities measured in the new units. If we are told that a room is 15 ft. by 20 ft., we have no problem in visualizing the dimensions of the room, thanks to our familiarity with the old British units. But if we are told that a room is 5 m by 7,5 m, it is not easy at first to visualize the dimensions of the room. Because of this difficulty, we are inclined to use dimensions in the old British units and then multiply them by the conversion factors given in Table 5 (at the end of the chapter) in order to obtain the equivalent dimensions in SI units. For example, since a foot is shown in Table 5 to be equal to 0,305 m, we find that a 15-by-20-ft. room is

$$15 \times 0,305 \text{ m by } 20 \times 0,305 \text{ m, or roughly } 4,5 \text{ m} \times 6,0 \text{ m.}$$

I would like to suggest that, particularly at first, you do not use the conversion factors. Instead, try to guess physical dimensions in SI units. This may feel difficult at first, but it will enable you to get used to the SI units much faster. (Of course, after having guessed the dimensions in SI units, check your guess by means of the factors.) You will be surprised at how soon you become sensitive to the physical meaning of the SI units. (I speak from experience. When I arrived in the United States from Europe, I had to learn the physical meaning of the old British units, because I used the metric system in my native country.) You should adopt the SI system from now on and express the values of all the quantities and dimensions of Math Camp 14 in the new units.

Math Camp
14

Try to guess the solution of the problems in this Math Camp (chosen from those in Math Camp 13), using physical approximations to the SI dimensions. Then check the approximate results obtained by using the conversion factors given in Table 5.

For example,

1 Compute the length of your arm in meters.

a) Guess the length of your arm to be 1 m.

b) Measure your arm length with a British-unit tape measure. Assume that it is equal to 35 in. From the conversion factor in Table 5, you would find:

35 in. = 35 × 25,4 mm = 889 / 1 000 m = 0,889 m ≈ 0,9 m. (The symbol ≈ means "almost equal to.") Your guess in SI units would not have been a bad approximation.

2 Compute the length of the front of your house in meters. (See Math Camp 13, problem 2.)

3 Compute the height of your building in meters. (See Math Camp 13, problem 3.)

4 A town's business district is a rectangle 100 ft. by 150 ft. Compute its area in square meters and in square dekameters.

5 Compute the volume of a cube with 12-in. sides in cubic centimeters and in cubic meters.

6 Compute, in °C, the temperature of a cup of coffee at 50°F.

7 Compute the average speed of a marathon winner who ran 26.2 mi. in 2 hr. 12 min., using km/hr and m/s.

8 Compute, using km/hr and m/s, the average speed of a plane that flew 3,000 mi. in 6 hr.

9 Compute the water flow in problem 10 of Math Camp 13, using liters per day.

10 Compute the cost of the concrete needed to fill the trench in problem 13 of Math Camp 13, in dollars and in Italian lire at 1 500 lire to the dollar.

Table 5   Conversion Factors from British to SI Units

	British Units		SI Units		
Length	mile	=	km	×	1,609
	yard	=	m	×	0,914
	foot	=	m	×	0,305
	inch	=	mm	×	25,4
Area	square mile	=	km^2	×	2,590
	acre	=	m^2	×	4 047
	square yard	=	m^2	×	0,836
	square foot	=	m^2	×	0,092 9
	square inch	=	mm^2	×	645
Volume	cubic foot	=	m^3	×	0,028 3
	cubic yard	=	m^3	×	0,765
	cubic foot	=	cm^3	×	28 300
	gallon	=	liter (l)	×	3,79
	cubic inch	=	cm^3	×	16,387
	cubic inch	=	mm^3	×	16 387

Examples:
a) 15 mi.= 15 × 1, 609 km = 24,135 km
b) 24,135 km = (24,135/1,609) mi.= 15 mi.

Chapter 5

Plane Geometry

Geometry is the field of mathematics that deals with the shape and size of things. As such it influences all aspects of our lives. Geometry influences the arts and the sciences and helps us to see and understand our own world and the entire universe. The design of our cars, planes, and boats; the planning of our cities, buildings, and apartments; even of our own bedrooms involves geometry in all of its aspects.

Geometry is subdivided into two closely related fields of study, called **plane** or **two-dimensional** geometry and **space** or **three-dimensional** geometry. "Plane" means a flat surface such as the smooth top of a table. It should not be confused with "plain," which means simple or easily understood.

We will discuss both plane and space geometry in this and the following chapter. I am sure you will enjoy it because geometry can be lots of fun.

🎲 THE CIRCLE

The **circle** is a closed curve, lying in a plane, that has all of its points at the same distance from the point called its **center** (Fig. 13). A line segment connecting a point on the circle to the center is called a **radius** of the circle.

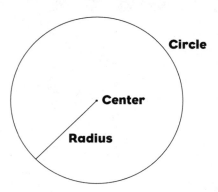

Figure 13 A circle is a closed curve in a plane, where all points on the circle lie at the same distance, called the radius, from the center of the circle.

A line segment connecting two opposite points on the circle and passing through the center (a distance of two **radii**) is called the **diameter** of the circle. The distance around a circle is called its **circumference,** and the **area** of a circle is the surface bound by the circumference (Fig. 14). You see circles all around you; one of the first examples that comes to mind is the outer shape of a car wheel.

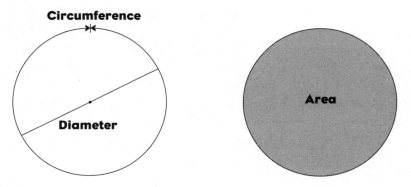

Figure 14 **Circumference** is the distance around the circle. A **diameter** is any straight line passing through the center and connecting opposite points. **Area** is the amount of surface inside the circle.

You probably feel that, once you have the length of the radius of a circle, it would be easy to determine the length of its circumference. After all, even if you do not have a compass (a device to draw circles), you can press a tack into a wooden tablet, connect one end of a string to it and the other end to a pencil, and draw a circle by rotating the pencil around the nail (Fig. 15). (It takes a

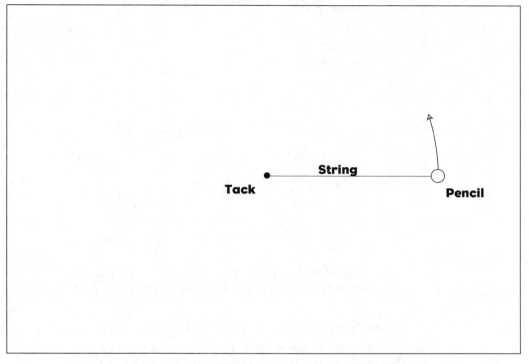

Paper with board under it.

Figure 15 Place paper on a wooden board. Push a tack through the paper into the board. Tie one end of a string to the tack, the other end to a pencil. Draw a circle on the paper with the pencil.

little practice to keep the string taut and the pencil vertical while smoothly drawing a complete circle.)

Yet it took mathematicians centuries to figure out that in order to obtain the exact length of the circumference of a circle, one must multiply the length of its radius by a number that has an unending number of decimal figures that follow one another at random. (We call such numbers **irrational**.)

The Greeks, who were the great geometers of 2,500 years ago, called this number **pi** and represented it by π, which is the Greek letter for "p," the first letter of "perimeter." To get an approximate value for π, measure the circumference c of a can and then the diameter d of its top (Fig. 16). You will find that the ratio of the circumference divided by the diameter (c/d) is the same value (at least approximately), whatever the size of the can (assuming you have an undamaged can). This value is π.

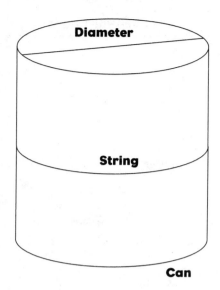

Figure 16 Estimate π by dividing the circumference (length of string around can) by the diameter of the top.

In the Bible π is said to be 3. The Egyptians computed it over 3,000 years ago to be about 3.16. Archimedes, the great Greek mathematician of 200 B.C., approximated π by the fraction 22/7 = 3.1428, which is accurate to two decimal digits. But the Chinese mechanical expert Tsu Ch'ung-chih, in 470 A.D., gave an even better approximation of π, involving the first three odd numbers, 1, 3, and 5, by means of the fraction 355/113 = 3.1415929, which is correct to six decimal digits. (The first dozen decimal digits of π are 3.14159265358, and they go on and on.)

For your daily needs you can assume π to be 3.14. Sometimes the fraction 22/7 is handy instead. If you want to be more accurate, use 3.1416. But I want you to know that a British amateur mathematician, Mr. William Shanks, set up a computing office in 1858 to get the first 707 decimal digits of π. It took 15 years of hand calculations (there were no computers then). The sad end of Mr. Shanks' story is that, in 1945, a mistake was found in his calculations; his results after the first 527 decimal digits were wrong.

Recently, two Russian mathematicians working at Columbia University borrowed $75,000 from their wives and built a special computer. With this computer, they were able to evaluate the first 2 billion 200 million decimal figures of π. You may think they were crazy because nobody would ever need to know π with that kind of accuracy, but they were not. Their purpose was to show that, with a relatively small amount of money, a computer could be built that would guarantee such incredible accuracy. (We know that, at the present time [1996], a Japanese computer expert is working hard to beat the Russians' accuracy, and may soon succeed.)

Once the value of π is determined to the needed accuracy (which we will assume from now on to be 3.14), the following formulas give the circumference c and area a of a circle with radius r or diameter $d = 2r$:

$$c = 2\pi r = \pi d \qquad\qquad (1)$$
$$a = \pi r^2 = (1/4)\,\pi d^2. \qquad\qquad (2)$$

For example, if your watch has a diameter of 1 inch, its area is:

$$a = (1/4) \times 3.14 \times 1^2 = 0.785 \text{ sq. in.}$$

If the wheel of your bike has a radius of 0.75 feet, its circumference is:

$$c = 2 \times 3.14 \times 0.75 = 4.71 \text{ ft.} \qquad\qquad (3)$$

so that, for each time your wheel rotates, you move ahead 4.71 feet.

If you divide the area of a circle into four equal parts by drawing two diameters perpendicular to one another, you get four **quadrants** of a circle (Fig. 17). Such quadrants are subdivided by means of radii into 90 equal angles called **degrees** that are symbolized by a small raised circle °. So an entire circle consists of $4 \times 90° = 360°$.

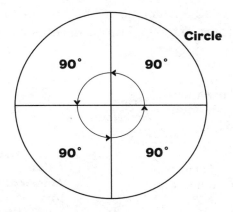

Figure 17 Four quadrants of a circle, obtained by drawing two diameters at 90° to one another, thereby dividing the circle into four equal parts.

A protractor, a semicircular instrument made of plastic or steel and marked with a degree scale, can be used to measure or draw angles, usually starting at the right end of a horizontal diameter and moving around the circle counterclockwise; that is, in a direction opposite to that of the hands of a clock (Fig. 18).

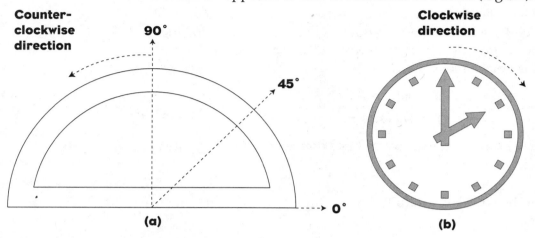

(a)   **(b)**

Figure 18 (a) A protractor, used to measure and draw angles.
(b) A clock, showing clockwise direction of hands.

A circle is often used to allow the visualization of percentages; that is to say, of fractions of quantities like the population of a country or the results of an election. For example, if we divide the area of a circle into four equal parts by means of two diameters at right angles, each part represents 1/4 or 25/100 (25%) of the total area (100%) of the circle.

Fig. 19 is a **circular graph** of the results of a population survey, which determined that the population of an American city consisted of 10% Asian Americans, 20% African Americans, 30% Hispanic Americans, and 40% European Americans.

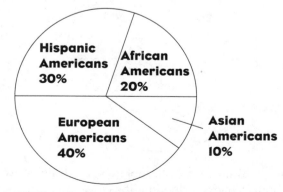

Figure 19 Circular graph showing results of a population survey of a city.

The area of the circle corresponding to the full 360° is subdivided by radii in proportion to the population percentages:

$10\% \times 360° = (10/100) \times 360° = 36°$ for the Asian Americans;
$20\% \times 360° = (20/100) \times 360° = 72°$ for the African Americans;
$30\% \times 360° = (30/100) \times 360° = 108°$ for the Hispanic Americans;
$40\% \times 360° = (40/100) \times 360° = 144°$ for the European Americans.

A circular graph makes it easy to visualize the population ratios and gives one an immediate understanding of their meaning. You will learn how to draw circular graphs and appreciate their usefulness when solving the problems of Math Camp 15.

Math 🔥 Camp
15

Assume π to be equal to 3.14 in all the following problems.

1 A park in your city has a circular lake 4 feet deep with a radius of 50 feet. It is surrounded by a circular footpath 4 feet wide (Fig. 20).

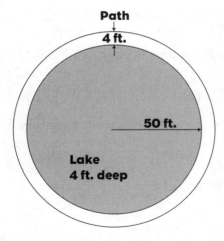

Figure 20 Math Camp 15, problem 1.

   a) How many cubic feet of water does the lake contain?

   b) How many feet do you walk along the entire inner side of the circular path in a stroll around the lake?

   c) How many feet do you walk along the entire outer side of the footpath?

2 The plaza in front of St. Peter's church in Rome, Italy, includes a large circular area partly surrounded by a portico of double columns on opposite sides of the circle (Fig. 21).

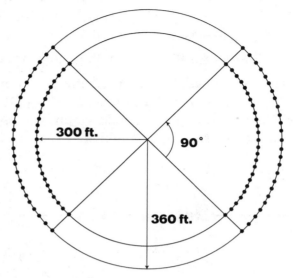

Figure 21 Math Camp 15, problem 2.

Each side has 50 columns; 25 are equally spaced on a quarter-circle of radius 300 feet and 25 are equally spaced on a quarter-circle of radius 360 feet.

a) What is the angle between two radii from the center of the plaza and two adjacent inner columns?

b) What is the area of the inner circle in square feet?

c) What is the length of one inner row of columns?

d) What is the length of one outer row of columns?

3 The round portholes of a passenger boat have an inner diameter of 1.5 feet. What is the area of each porthole?

4 A musical carousel has wooden horses turning in a circle at a radius of 20 feet and a wooden platform extending 2 feet beyond the circle of horses. What is the area occupied by the carousel?

5 The tunnel under the British Channel (called the Chunnel) has a round cross-sectional shape with a radius of 70 feet. It is 30 miles long. What is the surface area of the Chunnel? (A mile is 5,280 feet.)

6 A can of soup has a diameter of 3 inches and a height of 4.5 inches. How many square inches of tin are needed to build the can?

7 The circular bottom of a cooking pot has an area of 50 square inches. What is the diameter of the cooking pot?

8 A circular swimming pool has a radius of 10 feet and is 6 feet deep. How many cubic feet of water does it contain?

9 Measure the circumference of your wrist with a measuring tape and compute its cross-sectional area, assuming that your wrist has a circular cross section.

10 Into how many parts do you divide the area of a circle by means of radii 36° apart from each other and by radii 51.43° apart?

11 Measure the length of a toothpick. On an 8 1/2-by-11-inch sheet of paper, draw equally spaced lines parallel to the short side of the paper. Make the distance between the lines equal to the length of the toothpick (Fig. 22).

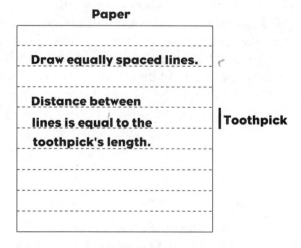

Figure 22 Math Camp 15, problem 11.

Throw the toothpick on the lined sheet of paper a number of times. Calculate the ratio, R, of the number of times the toothpick crosses a line divided by the number of times the toothpick is thrown. You will find that the greater the number of times you throw the toothpick on the lined sheet of paper, the nearer the value $2/R$ will be to π:

$$2/R \rightarrow \pi ,$$

where the arrow indicates that the quantity on the left, $2/R$, is approaching the value $\pi = 3.14$ on the right. To save time and get a good estimate of π, throw 10 toothpicks each time and go up to 20, 30, or even 50 throws. (Can you see why this ratio approaches π? It is not easy.)

🎲 THE TRIANGLE

A closed figure with straight sides is called a **polygon.** A polygon is called **regular** if all its sides are equal and the sides meet at equal angles. Fig. 23 shows the first four regular polygons.

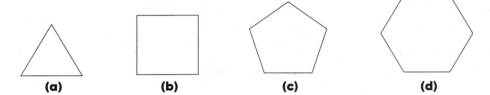

Figure 23 The first four regular polygons:
(a) equilateral triangle (b) square (c) regular pentagon (d) regular hexagon.
All sides of a regular polygon have the same length, and all interior angles are equal.

The polygon with the smallest number of sides is the **triangle.** Fig. 24 shows the names with which we label different kinds of triangles, according to the number of equal sides: **equilateral** if all three sides are equal (and hence three equal angles); **isosceles,** if only two sides are equal (and hence two equal angles); **scalene,** if the three sides are different (and hence three different angles).

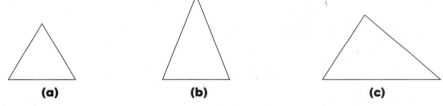

Figure 24 Types of triangles, named according to the number of equal sides:
(a) equilateral (3 sides equal). (b) isosceles (2 sides equal). (c) scalene (no sides equal).

All triangles, whatever their shape, have one property in common: their three interior angles always add up to 180°, as shown in the example in Fig. 25.

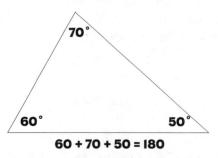

60 + 70 + 50 = 180

Figure 25 The three interior angles of a triangle add up to 180°.

So the three angles of an equilateral triangle are always equal to $180°/3 = 60°$. For an isosceles triangle, if the unequal angle is measured and found to be $\alpha°$ (α is the Greek letter for a), each of the other two equal angles is:

$$(180° - \alpha°)/2.$$

For example, the isosceles triangle of Fig. 26, with one angle $\alpha° = 40°$, has two other angles of:

$$(180° - 40°)/2 = 140°/2 = 70°.$$

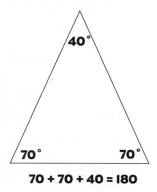

Figure 26 Example of an isosceles triangle. (Interior angles add up to 180°.)

One of the most frequently met triangles is the **right** triangle, which has one angle equal to 90° (Fig. 27a). A right triangle that is also isosceles has a 90° angle and two 45° angles (Fig. 27b).

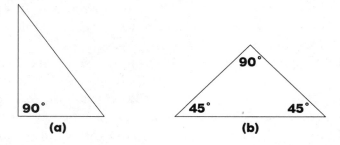

Figure 27 (a) A right triangle has one angle equal to 90°. (b) An isosceles right triangle.

It is the glory of the Greek mathematician Pythagoras (582–507 B.C.) to have proven for any right triangle that the sum of the squares of the two sides joining at a right angle equals the square of the third side. The third side, opposite the 90° angle, is called the **hypotenuse** of the right triangle. For example, in the right triangle of Fig. 28, with sides of 5 and 12 units and a hypotenuse of 13 units:

$$5^2 + 12^2 = 25 + 144 = 169 = 13^2.$$

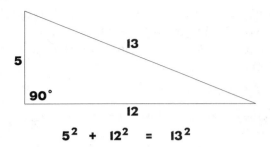

$$5^2 + 12^2 = 13^2$$

Figure 28 For any right triangle, the sum of the squares of the two sides joining at 90° is equal to the square of the third side (hypotenuse). This is called the Pythagorean theorem.

There are an infinite number of right triangles with whole-number sides that satisfy Pythagoras's theorem. (Two such triangles are 8, 15, 17 and 20, 21, 29; check and see.) The simplest and most famous is the 3, 4, 5 triangle:

$$3^2 + 4^2 = 9 + 16 = 25 = 5^2.$$

Some people believe that the Egyptians must have used the 3, 4, 5 triangle nearly 5,000 years ago to draw the accurate right angles at the square bases of their pyramids.

On the other hand, a right triangle with whole-number sides 3 and 5 does not have a whole-number hypotenuse because:

$$3^2 + 5^2 = 9 + 25 = 34 = 5.831^2.$$

Mathematicians refer to any whole number as an **integer,** whether it is positive, negative, or zero. For example, 1, 5, –4, 0, and –137 are all integers.

Pythagoras's theorem is perhaps the most famous theorem of geometry and one of the most famous in the entire field of mathematics, for a very strange reason. Ever since Pythagoras proved his theorem around 500 B.C., mathematicians the world over have wondered whether his equation with integer exponents larger than 2 has positive integer answers. (Negative and zero answers are not allowed.) For example, could positive integers a, b, c be found such that:

$$a^3 + b^3 = c^3 ?$$

Or how about higher exponents? It was just the kind of investigation to attract a pure mathematician. Yet, despite the research done by hundreds of mathematicians (many of them among the greatest), and despite the many proposed solutions (all eventually proved wrong), no answers could be found that satisfied

Pythagoras's equation with integer sides and exponents larger than 2! Mathematicians continued searching until, more than 2,000 years after Pythagoras's death, Pierre de Fermat (1601–1665) came along. Fermat made his living as a lawyer (he was even a counselor to the king of France). But he was attracted to mathematics and in his spare time he became a top-notch mathematician. In one of his Greek math books, he wrote in the margin that he had found a "wonderful proof that Pythagoras's equation cannot be satisfied with integer answers and exponents larger than 2, but the margin of the book is too narrow to contain it." His statement, known as **Fermat's last theorem,** became famous, and the best mathematicians in the world tried to prove it. But all the proposed proofs were shown to be wrong until, in 1993, 350 years after Fermat's assertion, Professor Andrew Wiles of Princeton University, after eight years dedicated exclusively to the solution of the darned theorem (and with a final push from Professor Richard Taylor of Cambridge University, one of his former students), proved Fermat's last theorem to his own glory and to the joy of a relieved mathematical world.

I was eager to tell you this story to show you that mathematics can be so fascinating as to drive some people to heroic efforts and years of hard work for no other reason than the pleasure of solving an extremely difficult problem. I also wanted you to know about the recent happy ending of a saga that lasted more than 300 years, lest one of you might decide to try to prove Fermat's last theorem yourself! (Let me add that most mathematicians alive today believe that Fermat's "wonderful proof" must have been wrong.)

Remembering that the area of a rectangle is obtained by multiplying the lengths of its two perpendicular sides (width times height), it is easy to figure out how to compute the area of a triangle. First, look at a right triangle, which means a triangle with two perpendicular sides. Its area is half of a rectangle, as shown in Fig. 29, so the area of a right triangle is equal to half the product of its two perpendicular sides.

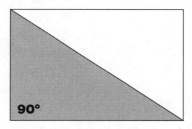

Figure 29 The area of a right triangle is half the area of a rectangle.

For example, if one of the perpendicular sides is 4 inches and the other is 6 inches, then the right triangle's area, *a*, is:

$$a = (1/2)\,(4 \times 6) = 12 \text{ sq. in.}$$

Given a general triangle, shown in Fig. 30, we can separate it into two right triangles by drawing, from **vertex** A, a line perpendicular to the base BC.

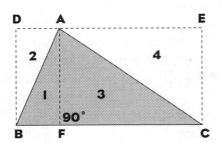

Figure 30 The area of any triangle is half the area of a rectangle (because triangles 1 and 2 have the same area, and so do triangles 3 and 4).

Now draw the dotted lines of the rectangle BDEC that touches the **vertices** A, B, and C. Since the areas of triangles 1 and 2 are equal, as are those of triangles 3 and 4, the area of triangle ABC is equal to half the area of the rectangle BDEC. (You may prove this to yourself as follows. Draw any triangle ABC inside the edges of a rectangle made of paper, as in Fig. 30. Then cut triangles 2 and 4 from the rectangle, leaving triangle ABC. Then rotate these two triangles so they cover triangle ABC.)

The perpendicular AF to the side BC is called the **height,** *h,* of the triangle, and the side BC is the **base,** *b*. So the area, *a*, of any triangle is half its base times its height, or:

$$a = (1/2)\,(b \times h).$$

For the isosceles triangle of Fig. 31, with two sides of length 3 inches and a base 4 inches long, we first calculate the height, *h,* by applying Pythagoras's theorem to one of the two right triangles.

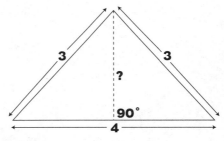

Figure 31 How do you calculate the height of this isosceles triangle? (Hint: use symmetry.)

By symmetry, the base of either right triangle is half the base of the isosceles triangle, so:

$$(4/2)^2 + h^2 = 3^2; h^2 = 9 - 4 = 5 \text{ sq. in.}; h = \sqrt{5} = 2.236 \text{ in.}$$

Then the isosceles triangle's area, a, is:

$$a = (1/2)\, 4 \times h = 2h = 4.472 \text{ sq. in.}$$

A completely different way to compute the area of a triangle was discovered by the Greeks more than 2,000 years ago. It is called Heron's formula (sometimes called Hero's formula). First, measure the lengths of the three sides, x, y, z. The **perimeter** of a triangle is the sum of its sides: $x + y + z$. The area, a, can be calculated from the **semiperimeter,** $s = (x + y + z)/2$, using:

$$a = \sqrt{s(s-x)(s-y)(s-z)}.$$

For example, for the isosceles triangle of Fig. 31, $s = (4 \text{ in.} + 3 \text{ in.} + 3 \text{ in.})/2 = 5 \text{ in.}$, so its area is:

$$a = \sqrt{5(5-4)(5-3)(5-3)} = 4.472 \text{ sq. in.}$$

This is the same area we found by first using Pythagoras's theorem to find the height and then calculating the area as half the product of the base and the height.

(Given the lengths of the three sides of a general triangle, its height, h, can also be computed with more advanced knowledge of mathematics, using **trigonometry** and **quadratic equations.** However, using a ruler and compass, you may find a good estimate of h by drawing a scaled version of the triangle, drawing and measuring the scaled triangle's height, and scaling this height back to the original size.)

Math 🌱 Camp
16

Check the results of the problems in this Math Camp by folding a square piece of paper into an isosceles triangle, whenever the involved triangle is isosceles.

1 A small town has a triangular town square with its smallest angle equal to 35° and the next-larger angle of 60°. Determine the value of its largest angle.

2 An isosceles triangle has two 45° angles. Determine the value of its third angle.

3 A right triangle has two perpendicular sides 7 inches long. How long is its third side?

4 An isosceles triangle has two sides of 5 inches and a base of 8 inches. What is the height to the base? What is the perimeter, the semiperimeter, and the area?

5 A rectangular sheet of paper has sides 8 1/2 by 11 inches long. How long are its diagonals?

6 A square street block has four equal sides 100 feet long. Determine the length of one diagonal of the block.

7 The facade of a church is shaped like an isosceles triangle with two sides 60 feet long and its base 50 feet long. Determine the height of the facade and its area.

8 A ladder, 6 feet long, is leaning with its top against a wall. The foot of the ladder rests on the floor 4 feet from the wall. How high above the floor is the top of the ladder?

9 A wooden right triangle used in drafting has one side 4 inches long and the other 6 inches long. How long is the triangle's hypotenuse? What is the area of the triangle?

10 Three steel brackets support a balcony 2 feet wide. The vertical side of each bracket is 2.5 feet long (Fig. 32). How long is the inclined side of each bracket?

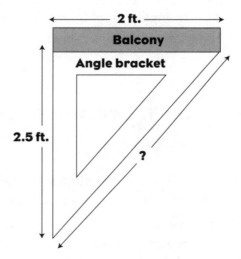

Figure 32 Math Camp 16, problem 10.

THE QUADRILATERALS

A **quadrilateral** is a closed geometrical plane (two-dimensional) figure with four straight sides; that is, it is a polygon with four sides (Fig. 33). It has two **diagonals,** which are the straight lines connecting opposite vertices. The **perimeter** is the sum of the lengths of the four sides.

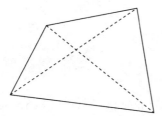

Figure 33 An arbitrary quadrilateral (a polygon with 4 sides). Its diagonals are the two straight lines connecting opposite vertices (dotted lines).

Fig. 34 shows the names with which we label some of the most common quadrilaterals. The **rectangle** has two pairs of parallel sides at right angles to one another; the **square** is a rectangle with four equal sides; the **parallelogram** has two pairs of parallel sides not at right angles to one another (a "lazy rectangle"); the **rhombus** is a parallelogram with four equal sides not at right angles (a "lazy square"); and the **trapezoid** has two unequal sides parallel to one another.

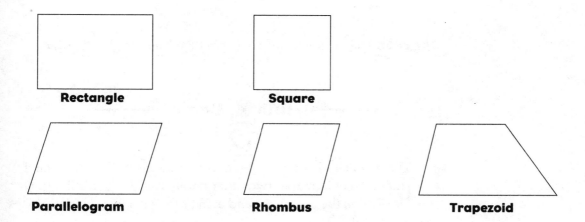

Figure 34 Different types of quadrilaterals.

You know that the area of a rectangle is equal to the product of its base times its height. But did you know that the area of a parallelogram (and therefore a rhombus) is also the product of the base b times the height h, as shown in Fig. 35? (Prove this to yourself mentally, by cutting right triangle 1 off the left side and placing it on top of right triangle 2, making a rectangle.)

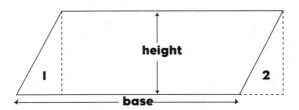

Figure 35 The area of a parallelogram is the base times the height (the same as the rectangle formed by cutting off right triangle 1 and placing it over triangle 2).

The area, a, of an **irregular** quadrilateral may be obtained as the sum of the areas of two triangles, by drawing either one of the two diagonals, thereby splitting the quadrilateral into two triangles. For example, using the numbers given in Fig. 36:

$$a = (1/2)(6 \times 1) + (1/2)(6 \times 2) = 3 + 6 = 9 \text{ sq. in.}$$

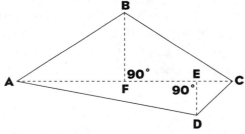

Figure 36 Diagonal AC = 6 in. Height BF = 2 in. Height DE = 1 in.

──────── Math 🔥 Camp ────────
17

1 The business district of a town is a rectangle with two parallel sides 90 feet long and two other parallel sides 120 feet long. Determine the perimeter and area of the business district.

2 A town square has sides 40 feet long. Determine the perimeter, the area, and the length of the diagonal of this square.

3 A parallelogram has two parallel sides 100 feet long and two other parallel sides 80 feet long. The two longer sides are 60 feet apart. Determine the perimeter and the area of the parallelogram.

4 Determine the area of a square that is 4 inches by 4 inches, but do it "the hard way," by drawing a diagonal, computing its length, and then computing the area of the two triangles formed by the diagonal. (Hint: Since we are talking about a square, the other diagonal is perpendicular to the one you drew, and it has the same length.)

5 The parallelogram in Fig. 37 has base b and height h. Evaluate its area and draw a square with the same area as the parallelogram.

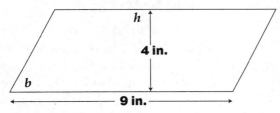

Figure 37 Math Camp 17, problem 5.

6 A kite-shaped quadrilateral is made from two identical triangles as shown in Fig. 38. Determine its perimeter and its area.

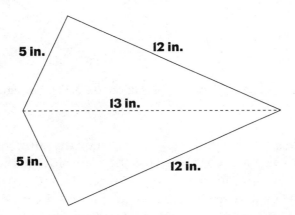

Figure 38 Math Camp 17, problem 6.

7 An irregular quadrilateral has four sides of lengths 8 inches, 12 inches, 9 inches, and 17 inches and diagonal of 15 inches, as shown in Fig. 39. What is its perimeter and its area? (Hint: Use Pythagoras's theorem to convince yourself that the quadrilateral is actually made up of two right triangles; then compute the areas.)

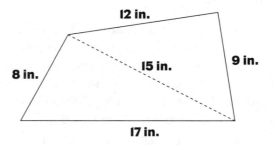

Figure 39 Math Camp 17, problem 7.

🎲 THE REGULAR POLYGONS

Regular polygons are polygons with equal sides making equal angles between two adjacent sides. We have already met two regular polygons, the equilateral triangle and the square. Fig. 40 introduces the **pentagon,** with five equal sides, the **hexagon,** with six equal sides, the **octagon,** with eight equal sides (a stop sign has this shape), and the **dodecagon,** with 12 equal sides.

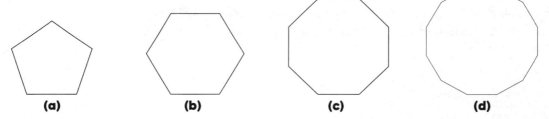

(a)　　　　**(b)**　　　　**(c)**　　　　**(d)**

Figure 40 Regular polygons: (a) pentagon (5 sides) (b) hexagon (6 sides) (c) octagon (8 sides) (d) dodecagon (12 sides).

All regular polygons can be drawn by dividing the area of a circle into as many equal parts as there are sides to the polygons. Fig. 41 shows the special angles between the radii of the circle that allow us to **inscribe** the polygons in the circle: $360°/3 = 120°$ for the equilateral triangle; $360°/4 = 90°$ for the square; $360°/5 = 72°$ for the pentagon; $360°/6 = 60°$ for the hexagon; $360°/8 = 45°$ for the octagon; and $360°/12 = 30°$ for the dodecagon. The hexagon is unique among all regular polygons because it is composed of six equilateral triangles whose sides equal the radius of the **circumscribed** circle.

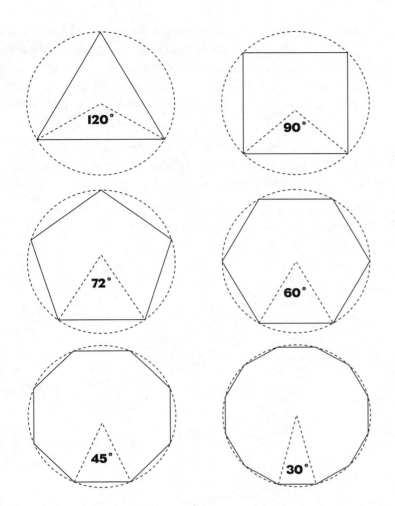

Figure 41 Regular polygons inscribed in circles. The size of the central angle (between radii through adjacent vertices) depends on the number of sides.

—————— Math 🔥 Camp ——————
18

1 Using a compass, draw six circles with a radius of 4 inches on six sheets of paper. Inscribe an equilateral triangle, a square, a regular pentagon, a regular hexagon, a regular octagon, and a regular dodecagon in each of the six circles (Fig. 41).

2 Measure the side of each regular polygon in problem 1 and add the length of their sides touching the circle to obtain the perimeters of the regular polygons. Divide the perimeters by the diameter (8 in.) and compare the results with π. (The Greeks approximated π by calculating the perimeters of the regular polygons with over 300 sides.)

3 A hexagon is inscribed in a circle of radius 2 inches. Compute the area of the hexagon and determine the side of the square with the same area as the hexagon.

4 A rectangle has a base of 8 feet and a height of 2 feet. Determine the length of the side of the square with the same area as the rectangle.

■ ■ ■ ■ ■ ■ ■ ■ ■ ■ ■ ■ ■ ■ ■ ■ ■

Chapter

Space Geometry

🎲 OUR SPACE

The space in which we live has three dimensions, usually labeled **length, width,** and **height.** Hence, **three-dimensional,** or **space, geometry** is essential in describing most of the objects we build and the dimensions and shapes of the space in which we move.

Let us start looking at three-dimensional geometry by noticing that we can create many different three-dimensional figures by moving the two-dimensional figures of plane geometry (Chapter Five) through space.

🎲 SPACE FIGURES GENERATED BY PLANE FIGURES

If you twirl a circle around one of its diameters, you get a three-dimensional closed surface called a **sphere,** whose points are all at the same distance from its center (Fig. 42).

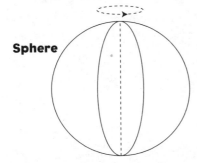

Figure 42 Twirling a circle around a diameter produces a surface in space called a sphere. All points on the sphere are the same distance from the center of the circle.

The sphere is one of the most common and familiar shapes around us. To begin with, we live on the surface of the earth, which is an almost perfect sphere with a radius of about 4,000 miles. We think the earth is big, but the sun, which sends us the light and heat we need to live, is also a sphere (composed of hot gases) with a radius of 432,000 miles, 108 times the size of the earth.

Going from very large to fairly small spheres, basketballs are about 10 inches in diameter, soccer balls about 8.5 inches in diameter, and tennis balls about 2.5 inches in diameter.

When a steel sphere rolls on a smooth surface, it develops only a minimum amount of frictional resistance. This is why tiny steel balls are used in gadgets called ball bearings, which are utilized in almost all machines with rotating parts (such as the wheels of a car or bicycle).

Atoms, the basic elements of matter, consist of a nucleus surrounded by circling electrons, in a configuration that looks like a sphere with a diameter about one centimeter (0.4 inches) divided by 100,000,000 (one hundred million)!

By now, you are aware that spheres of all sizes play a very important role in our lives.

Since a sphere is generated by twirling a circle of radius r around one of its diameters, you will not be surprised to find out that π appears in the formula for its surface area, S:

$$S = 4\pi \times r^2$$

(which is four times the area of the generating circle); and its volume V:

$$V = (4/3)\,\pi \times r^3.$$

Other useful three-dimensional shapes can be generated with a circle, one of which I am sure you like very much. If you move the center of a vertical circle around the circumference of a larger horizontal circle, keeping the smaller circle perpendicular to the direction of the circumference, you create a surface in space that looks like a doughnut, which in geometry is called a **torus** (Fig. 43).

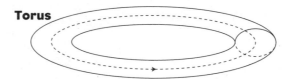

Torus

Figure 43 Moving the center of a vertical circle around the circumference of a larger horizontal circle creates a doughnut-shaped surface in space called a torus.

If you move the center of a circle along a straight line perpendicular to the circle, you get a **cylinder** (Fig. 44), which, if hollow, is a **pipe** and, if solid and straight, is a **column,** one of the most important elements in architectural construction.

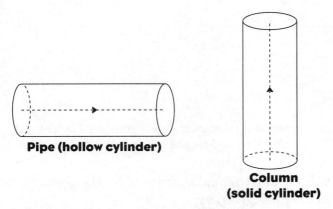

Pipe (hollow cylinder)

**Column
(solid cylinder)**

Figure 44 Moving the center of a circle along a straight line perpendicular to the circle creates a cylinder.

In the examples just mentioned, the pipe and the column, the volume V of these three-dimensional figures is given by the area A of the moving circle times the length h of its line. For example, the volume of a circular column of height h generated by a horizontal circle of radius r is given by:

$$V = \pi \times r^2 \times h.$$

Different three-dimensional figures can be generated by moving plane figures other than a circle. For example, moving a vertical square or a vertical rectangle horizontally, one obtains a square or a rectangular **prism** (Fig. 45).

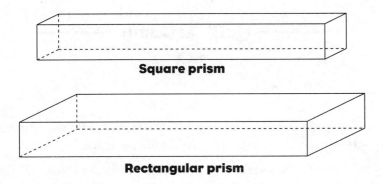

Square prism

Rectangular prism

Figure 45 Prisms generated by moving a vertical square or rectangle along horizontal straight lines.

By moving a vertical triangle horizontally, one generates a **triangular prism** (Fig. 46), which, if made of glass, splits sunlight into the colors of a rainbow (violet, indigo, blue, green, yellow, orange, and red), as first demonstrated by Isaac Newton in the 17th century.

Figure 46 Triangular prism generated by moving a vertical triangle along a horizontal straight line.

The volume of a triangular prism of length *h* generated by a triangle of area *A* is given by:

$$V = A \times h.$$

The volume and surface area of many other three-dimensional figures can be computed by a field of mathematics called the **calculus,** which you will encounter in a few years in high school. The calculus was invented simultaneously by Isaac Newton and by the German mathematician Gottfried Wilhelm von Leibniz. Since Newton did not publish his "theory of fluxions," as he called the calculus, Leibniz thought that Newton had plagiarized his discovery. As a result, a public feud exploded between these two great men and continued for several years, proving that even great mathematicians can behave like everyone else; that is, like simple human beings.

Math Camp

19

1   Compute the surface area of the earth and its volume using the square mile and the cubic mile as units.

2   Compute the surface area and the volume of the sun, using the square mile and the cubic mile as units.

3 Using the square inch and the cubic inch as units, compute the surface area and volume of:

a) a basketball;

b) a soccer ball;

c) a tennis ball.

4 A marble column has a circumference of 4 feet and is 15 feet tall. Compute its vertical surface area and its volume.

5 A triangular prism generated by an equilateral triangle (Fig. 46) with 1/2-inch sides is 10 inches long. Compute its surface area, including the surfaces of its two triangular bases, and its volume.

🎲 POLYHEDRA

A whole series of closed three-dimensional figures, called **poly-hedra** (from the Greek **poly,** meaning "many," and **hedra,** meaning "faces,") can be generated using polygons as faces. Since an infinite variety of polygons can be used, the number of poly-hedra is infinite. Yet the great Greek geometers of the fourth century B.C. discovered that, if all faces of a polyhedron are identical regular polygons (see Chapter Five, Section 4), only the five regular polyhedra of Fig. 47 can be put together.

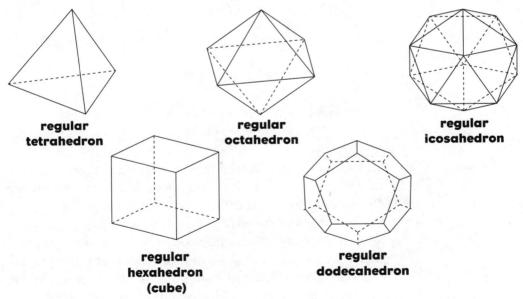

regular tetrahedron

regular octahedron

regular icosahedron

regular hexahedron (cube)

regular dodecahedron

Figure 47 The five regular polyhedra, called Platonic solids. The faces of each polyhedron are identical regular polygons. All faces of the top three are equilateral triangles, all faces of the cube are squares, and all faces of the regular dodecahedron are regular pentagons.

These five special polyhedra are called **Platonic solids,** although they were known before Plato, the great Greek philosopher who lived from 427 to 347 B.C. You might enjoy building the five Platonic solids out of paper, using tape or glue, starting with the simplest and ending with the most complicated, according to the suggestions in Math Camp 20.

Math Camp
20

1   **Regular tetrahedron.** The simplest **polyhedron** has just four faces and is called a **tetrahedron** (from the Greek **tetra,** for "four," and **hedron,** for "face"). A regular tetrahedron consists of four identical equilateral triangles. Although Fig. 48 may remind you of an Egyptian pyramid, which has a square base and four triangles on the sides, it is quite different. (In fact, the pyramid of Fig. 48 is one-half of an octahedron. Can you picture that in your mind?)

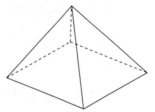

Figure 48 A pyramid; the base is square and the four side faces are triangles.

To build a regular tetrahedron, draw and cut out four identical equilateral triangles, joined together as shown in Fig. 49. (Or enlarge and duplicate Fig. 49 on a copying machine.) Make the edges of the triangles about 4 inches long. If all triangles cannot be drawn on one sheet of paper, they may be drawn on two or more sheets and then taped together. Carefully bend triangles 2, 3, and 4 up so that vertices A, B, and C meet at the top, above the center of the base triangle 1. You can tape the three open edges of the tetrahedron together with Scotch tape.

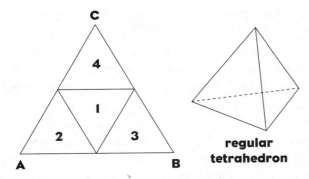

Figure 49 Math Camp 20, problem 1. Make a regular tetrahedron (4 faces, equilateral triangles).

2 **Regular hexahedron,** or cube. The next simplest regular polyhedron is the familiar cube (also called a regular **hexahedron,** from the Greek **hexa,** meaning "six"). Its six faces are identical squares. You may build one from paper by drawing and cutting out six identical squares, joined together as shown on the left of Fig. 50. (Or enlarge and duplicate Fig. 50 on a copying machine.) Make the edges of the squares about 4 inches long. If all squares cannot be drawn on one sheet of paper, they may be drawn on two or more sheets and then taped together. Square 1 is the base, squares 2, 3, 4, and 5 are the side faces, and square 6 is the top face of the cube. Carefully bend up the side faces and tape the four vertical edges together with Scotch tape. Then bend the top face down and tape the three horizontal edges together.

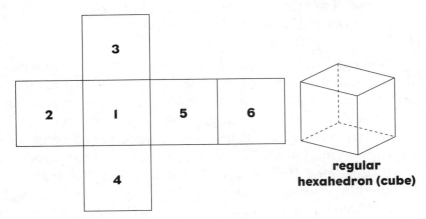

Figure 50 Math Camp 20, problem 2. Make a regular hexahedron (6 faces, identical squares): a cube.

3 **Regular octahedron.** A regular octahedron (from the Greek **octa,** for "eight,") has eight faces, all of which are identical equilateral triangles. To build one, draw and cut out eight equilateral triangles, joined together as shown in Fig. 51. (Or enlarge and duplicate Fig. 51 on a copying machine.) Make the edges of the triangles about 3 inches long. If all triangles cannot be drawn on one sheet of paper, they may be drawn on two or more sheets and then taped together. Carefully bend triangles 1, 2, and 3 up until the open adjacent edges of triangles 1 and 2 can be taped together. (Triangles 1, 2, 3, and 4 form a pyramid, Fig. 48.) Similarly, bend triangles 6, 7, and 8 up until the open adjacent edges of triangles 7 and 8 can be taped together. (Triangles 5, 6, 7, and 8 also form a pyramid.) Then tape the remaining open edges together. (In other words, tape the edges of the two pyramids together; these are the edges between triangles 3 and 8, 1 and 6, and 2 and 7.)

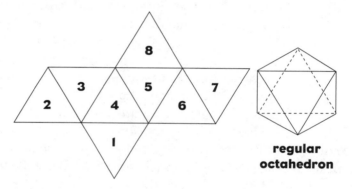

Figure 51 Math Camp 20, problem 3. Make a regular octahedron (8 faces, equilateral triangles).

4 **Regular dodecahedron.** A regular dodecahedron (from the Greek **dodeca,** for "twelve,") has 12 faces, all of which are identical regular pentagons. You may build one by drawing and cutting out 12 regular pentagons, joined together as shown in Fig. 52. (Or enlarge and duplicate Fig. 52 on a copying machine.) Make the edges of the pentagons about 3 inches long. If all pentagons cannot be drawn on one sheet of paper, they may be drawn on two or more sheets and then taped together. Pentagon 1 is the base, pentagon 12 is the top face, and pentagons 2, 3, . . . 11 are the side faces. Carefully bend up the side pentagons until the open adjacent edges can be taped together. In other words, tape the edges of pentagons 2 and 4 together; also 3 and 5, 4 and 6, 5 and 7, 6 and 8, 7 and 9, 8 and 10, 9 and 11. Then tape the edges of pentagons 2 and 10 together; also 3 and 11. Next tape the edges of the bottom pentagon to the edges of even-numbered pentagons. Then tape the edges of the top pentagon to the edges of the odd-numbered pentagons.

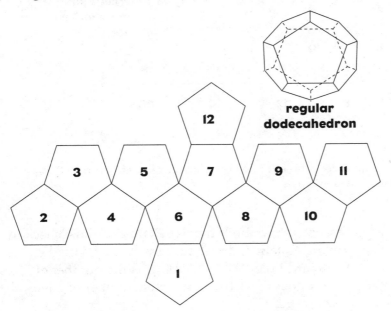

regular dodecahedron

Figure 52 Math Camp 20, problem 4. Make a regular dodecahedron (12 faces, identical regular pentagons).

5 **Regular icosahedron.** A regular icosahedron (from the Greek **icosa,** for "twenty,") has 20 faces, all of which are identical equilateral triangles. To build one, draw and cut out 20 equilateral triangles, joined together as shown in Fig. 53. (Or enlarge and duplicate Fig. 53 on a copying machine.) Make the edges of the triangles about 3 inches long. If all triangles cannot be drawn on one sheet of paper, they may be drawn on two or more sheets and then taped together. Carefully bend triangles 1, 2, 3, and 5 up until the open adjacent edges of triangles 1 and 5 meet and can be taped together. Proceed in a similar way with triangles 3, 4, 7, and 8, bending them up until the adjacent edges of triangles 4 and 8 can be taped together. Continue this way, bending up and taping the edges of triangles 5 and 9 together, then triangles 8 and 12, then 9 and 13, then 12 and 16, then 13 and 17, then 16 and 20. Finally, tape the edges of 20 and 4 together, then 19 and 2, then 17 and 1.

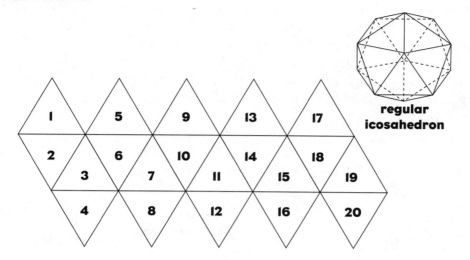

Figure 53 Math Camp 20, problem 5. Make a regular icosahedron (20 faces, equilateral triangles).

6 Once you have built the five Platonic solids, check the following equation, discovered by the Swiss mathematician Leonhard Euler (1707–1783). If f is the number of faces, v is the number of vertices, and e the number of edges, then $f + v = e + 2$.

Chapter

The Art of Graphing

 BAR GRAPHS

In Chapter Three you met the great French philosopher and mathematician René Descartes, who introduced the ingenious idea of exponents. I want you to meet him again for his greatest contribution to mathematics, the joining of **algebra** (the mathematics of numbers and equations) and geometry (the mathematics of shape). By combining geometry and algebra, Descartes gave us a way to see the abstractions of mathematics, thus allowing some of us to overcome the difficulties we have in dealing with abstract concepts.

One of the easiest ways of visualizing the numerical solution of some mathematical problems is by means of a **bar graph.** Here is an example of a bar graph that is probably used in your school.

Let us assume that your junior high school has three sixth-grade, two seventh-grade, and two eighth-grade classes of 30, 32, and 28 students each. The school principal, needing to know how many students are absent each day from each class, receives this information by means of the following numerical table:

April 9, 1995

6a	6b	6c	7a	7b	8a	8b
3	2	4	1	2	2	5

At the principal's request, the same information is now pre-sented by means of the bar graph of Fig. 54, which allows her to see at a glance the absence rates in each class.

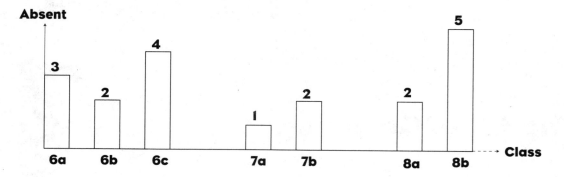

Figure 54 Bar graph showing the number of students absent in each class. The height of each bar is proportional to the number of students.

🎲 STRAIGHT LINES IN THE CARTESIAN PLANE

Descartes suggested the following procedure for locating a geo-metrical point on a plane with reference to two number lines at right angles to each other, called the **x-axis** and the **y-axis.** The x-axis is usually (but not necessarily) horizontal with its positive direction pointing to the right; the y-axis is usually (but not nec-essarily) vertical with its positive direction pointing upward (Fig. 55). The intersection of the x- and y-axes is called the origin and usually labeled O.

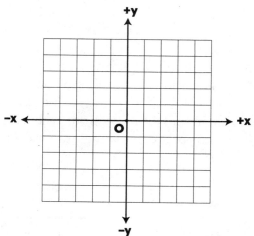

Figure 55 Cartesian plane showing x-axis (horizontal number line) and y-axis (vertical number line). The dot at $x = 0$, $y = 0$ is the origin (marked O).

Math Games for Middle School

Once units (not necessarily the same) are chosen for the two axes, a geometrical point is located on this plane by means of two numbers, called its **x and y coordinates**. These coordinates, which measure the number of horizontal and vertical units of the point from the two axes, are written in parentheses with the horizontal coordinate first, (x, y). The origin, corresponding to $x = 0$, $y = 0$, is $(0,0)$. Fig. 56 shows four such points, located by means of their (x, y) coordinates in the **Cartesian** plane (so named in honor of Descartes).

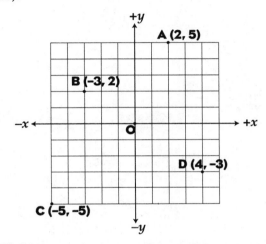

Figure 56 A graph showing four points A, B, C, D, and their (x, y) coordinates in the Cartesian plane.

Once you understand how to use Cartesian coordinates, you can not only locate a geometrical point on a plane, but also represent equations relating two quantities, x and y. For example, the equation:

$$y = 2x + 3 \qquad (1)$$

is a straight line in the Cartesian plane. You can see this by choosing different values of x, computing the corresponding values of y by means of equation (1), and graphing the coordinates of these points in the Cartesian plane. For example, from equation (1), we find:

if $x = 1$, then $y = 2 \times 1 + 3 = 5$.

Thus equation (1) generates the point with coordinates (1,5). Also from equation (1), we find:

if $x = 2$, then $y = 2 \times 2 + 3 = 7$.

So equation (1) generates the point (2,7). If we continue doing this for other values of x, we find that equation (1) generates points on the straight line through the two points (1,5) and (2,7), as shown in Fig. 57.

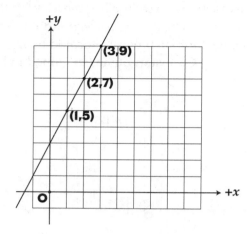

Figure 57 Graphing the equation $y = 2x + 3$ in the Cartesian plane generates a straight line.

For example, check equation (1) and you will see that, if $x = 3$, $y = 9$. Thus (3,9) is a point on the straight line, as shown in Fig. 57. The figure reveals the behavior of equation (1) at a glance. It also allows us to graph the value of y for any value of x. For example, run your eye up the y axis, which corresponds to $x = 0$, and you find the straight line intersecting the y-axis at $y = 3$, which means (0,3) is on the straight line. If you check equation (1), you will find this is so. Try a negative value such as $x = -1$ and you find (−1,1) on the line. The straight line and the equation correspond even when x is not an integer. For example, (1/2, 4) is on the straight line.

The Cartesian graph of two straight lines allows the solution of two **simultaneous linear equations** in two unknowns, x and y. (We will learn to solve such equations by means of algebra in the next chapter.) Given, for example, the two simultaneous equations:

$$2x + 3y = 8 \qquad\qquad (2)$$
$$3x + y = 5, \qquad\qquad (3)$$

we represent the straight lines of equations (2) and (3), as shown in Fig. 58, by the procedure explained above for equation (1).

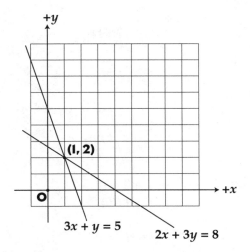

Figure 58 The intersection point (1, 2) of the two straight lines in the Cartesian plane is the simultaneous solution, $x = 1$, $y = 2$, of the two equations.

The point where the two lines **intersect** is (1,2), meaning $x = 1$ and $y = 2$. This is the solution of the simultaneous linear equations (2) and (3). You should check this by substituting these values into the two equations.

🎲 CURVED GRAPHS

The graphs of equations with higher powers of the two variables x and y represent curves instead of straight lines in the Cartesian plane. Visualizing such curves by means of graphing helps in understanding the behavior of two related quantities and in other practical applications of mathematical equations.

For example, Fig. 59 shows five points on the Cartesian curve of the equation:

$$y = x^2 + 2, \tag{4}$$

obtained by letting x equal 0, 1, 2, 3, 4 and computing the corresponding values of y by means of equation (4). Since $0^2 + 2 = 2$, we see that the point (0,2) is on the curve generated by equation (4). Likewise, since $2^2 + 2 = 6$, the point (2,6) is on the curve. To help visualize the curve, the five points have been connected by straight lines. A more accurate drawing of the curve would require more points. However, with just five points, you can clearly see that the curve of equation (4) curves up as x increases from $x = 0$.

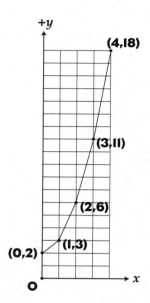

Figure 59 Five points generated by $y = x^2 + 2$ (connected by straight lines).

Fig. 60 shows five points (connected by straight lines) on the curve of the equation:

$$y = 1 - x^2. \tag{5}$$

Clearly the curve of equation (5) curves down as x increases from $x = 0$.

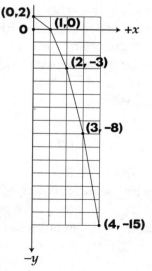

Figure 60 Five points generated by $y = 1 - x^2$ (connected by straight lines).

The graph of points generated by the equation:

$$y = 1 - 1/x^2 \qquad (6)$$

in Fig. 61 shows that as the value of x increases, the value of y grows, approaching the horizontal line at level $y = 1$ without ever reaching it. Such an approach is called **asymptotic,** and the horizontal line at level $y = 1$ is called the **asymptote** of equation (6).

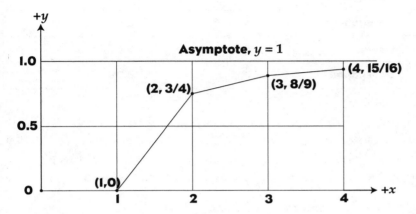

Figure 61 Four points generated by $y = 1 - 1/x^2$ (connected by straight lines). The curve approaches the asymptote, $y = 1$, without ever reaching it.

These three examples are typical of many physical phenomena, such as the temperature of an object being heated over a period of time (Fig. 59), of an object being cooled (Fig. 60), and of a cold one that is approaching the ambient temperature as it warms up (Fig. 61).

⬢ THE ASYMPTOTIC APPROACH TO π

Archimedes, the great mathematician and physicist of Greek antiquity, devised methods for calculating π very accurately. You used one of his methods in Math Camp 18, problem 2, where you inscribed regular polygons inside circles and measured the polygons' perimeters. When you divided the perimeters by the circles' diameters, you obtained numbers that approximate π, similar to those in Table 6.

Table 6

Inscribed Regular Polygon	Number of Sides	Perimeter divided by Diameter
Triangle	3	2.60
Square	4	2.83
Pentagon	5	2.94
Hexagon	6	3.00
Octagon	8	3.06
Dodecagon	12	3.09

You can see that the numbers in the right-hand column are getting closer and closer to 3.14 as the number of polygonal sides increases. This asymptotic approach to π is shown in Fig. 62, where Descartes's ingenious way of graphing is used.

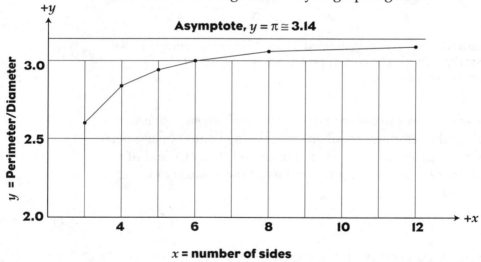

Figure 62 When regular polygons are inscribed in a circle, the ratio of the polygons' perimeters divided by the circle's diameter approaches (but never reaches) π as the number of polygonal sides increases. Thus π is an asymptote for this ratio. (Data are from Table 6.)

Archimedes (287–212 B.C.) lived about 1,900 years before Descartes and did not know about his clever way of visualizing numbers. But he understood the idea of getting closer and closer to a certain value without reaching it. You will see other examples of asymptotic approach to a value when we study probability in Chapter Ten.

THE CONCEPT OF SCALE

We have seen in Chapter Five that one may visualize the ratio of measured quantities by means of circular graphs, in which the values of such quantities are made proportional to the areas of the sections of a full circle (see Fig. 19).

The same approach can be used by dividing an area with a shape different from that of a circle into subareas proportional to the given quantities. Such two-dimensional graphs are particularly useful in mapping horizontal areas, like rooms, apartments, or land properties. They are made using the concept of **scale.**

Assume that your bedroom is to be built as a rectangle with sides of 10 feet by 15 feet and that the architect who is designing your apartment represents your room on a piece of drawing paper 12 inches by 18 inches. In order to represent your room on such a sheet of drawing paper, he had to choose a scale that would allow the representation of an area measuring 10 feet by 15 feet on an area measuring 12 inches by 18 inches. He may choose to represent 1 foot in the room by 1 inch on the drawing paper, so that your room will appear in the drawing as a rectangle 10 inches by 15 inches (Fig. 63). Such a drawing is said to be in the scale of 1 in. = 1 ft. (Fig. 63 was drawn to a smaller scale for this book.)

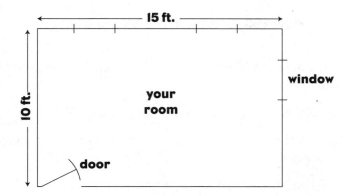

Figure 63 Architect's scaled drawing of a room with doors and windows.

Similarly, a rectangular piece of land with sides 200 feet by 600 feet may be represented at a scale of 1 in. = 20 ft. by drawing it in the shape of a rectangle 200/20 = 10 in. by 600/20 = 30 in. (Fig. 64). Other things such as a house and pond may be included. (Fig. 64 was drawn to a smaller scale for this book.)

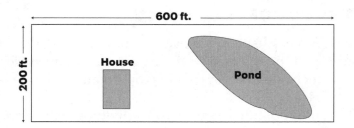

Figure 64 Scaled drawing of rectangular piece of land with house and pond.

Fig. 65 shows the map of a piece of land with an area of 200 acres. If it were drawn to the scale of 1 in. = 100 ft., then 1 sq. in. = 100^2 sq. ft. = 10,000 sq. ft.

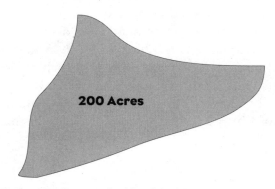

Figure 65 A parcel of land 200 acres in area.

Since 1 acre is 43,560 square feet, the land represented in Fig. 65 has an area of:

200 acres × 43,560 sq. ft. / acre = 8,712,000 sq. ft.,

and the scaled map (1 in. = 100 ft.) of that piece of land would have an area of:

8,712,000 sq. ft. / (10,000 sq. ft. / sq. in.) = 8,712,000 / 10,000 sq. in.
= 871.2 sq. in.

If the area of the land were square, the map would have a side of:

$$\sqrt{871.2} = 29.52 \text{ in.},$$

or about 2.5 feet.

1 The table below gives the Fahrenheit temperature at 12 noon during the first weeks of the months of May 1992 and May 1993. Present this data in the form of two bar graphs, one for each year.

	Mon	Tue	Wed	Thu	Fri	Sat	Sun
1992	56	60	52	57	50	51	49
1993	60	62	64	60	66	68	65

2 The table below gives the hourly value of a stock on the New York stock exchange during the hours of the stock exchange's operation (9 a.m. to 3 p.m.). Present these data in bar-graph form.

Time	9 a.m.	10 a.m.	11 a.m.	12 n.	1 p.m.	2 p.m.	3 p.m.
$	120	100	80	70	75	95	130

3 Locate the following points on the x,y plane by means of their Cartesian coordinates:

$$A (2,4), B (2,-1), C (-2,-4), D (0,5).$$

4 Draw the straight line representing the equation:

$$y = -3x + 4$$

between $x = 0$ and $x = 10$, using steps of 1 unit in the x and y directions.

5 Draw the straight line representing the equation:

$$y = 2x - 12$$

between $x = 0$ and $x = 10$, using steps of 1 unit in the x and y directions.

6 Draw the straight lines representing the two equations:

$$y = x \; ; y = 4$$

between $x = 0$ and $x = 10$, using steps of 1 unit in the x and y directions. At what point do these lines intersect?

7 Plot the graph of the equation:
$$y = x^2 - 1$$
between $x = 0$ and $x = 4$, using steps of 1 unit in the x and y directions.

8 Plot the graph of the equation:
$$y = x^2$$
between $x = 0$ and $x = 6$, using steps of 2 units in the x and y directions.

9 Plot the graph of the equation:
$$y = 2 - 1/x^2$$
between $x = 1$ and $x = 4$, using steps of 1 unit in the x direction and steps of $1/2 = 0.5$ in the y direction. This curve has an asymptote, since y gets closer and closer to a certain value as x increases. What is this asymptotic value? Draw the asymptote on your graph, and label it.

10 Your living room is 15 feet by 20 feet. Draw its plan at a scale of 1 in. = 2 ft.

11 The Leaning Tower of Pisa is cylindrical in shape, 50 feet in diameter, and 180 feet high. (The numbers given here are only approximate.) While it was being built, the ground underneath settled unevenly, causing it to lean. Its top edge on one side is now 179 feet above the ground. Use Pythagoras's theorem to find how far the top edge of the tower leans out above the edge of its base (Fig. 66). You may be surprised at how large this distance is, considering that the edge has dropped only 1 foot. Draw the Leaning Tower to a scale of 1 in. = 20 ft. (You could even go to the library and read about the Leaning Tower of Pisa.)

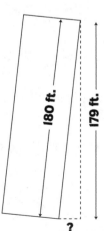

Figure 66 How far does the Leaning Tower of Pisa overhang the edge of its base?

12 At present (1995), the Verrazano Narrows bridge is the third-longest suspension bridge in the world and the longest in the United States (Fig. 67). It has a main span of 4,260 feet and two side spans of 1,214 feet each. Its two towers are 690 feet high. Draw the outline of the bridge at a scale of 1 in. = 200 ft.

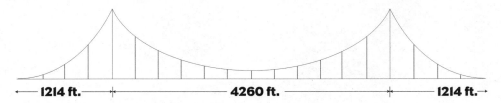

Figure 67 Math Camp 21, problem 12.

13 A piece of land has the rectangular shape shown in Fig. 64. Draw a map of the land at a scale of 1 in. = 30 ft. (You will need a large sheet of paper, or you may tape two standard sheets of paper together.) Determine the number of acres and write that information in the lower right-hand corner of the drawing (beneath the rectangle). Measure the house and pond in Fig. 64 and sketch them to scale on your map. Estimate the maximum length of the pond in feet and add that information to your drawing. Sign your drawing in the bottom right-hand corner (where architects often sign).

14 The radius of the earth is 4,000 miles. Draw a circle representing a cross section of the earth at a scale of 1 in. = 2,000 mi.

15 A building has 40 stories, each 9 feet high, and a facade 200 feet wide. Sketch the facade of the building at a scale of 1 in. = 24 ft.

Chapter 8

Simultaneous Linear Equations

 TWO QUESTIONS AND TWO ANSWERS

Yesterday you bought 10 oranges and 10 apples for $5.00. Today you bought five oranges and 12 apples, at the same unit prices, for $3.90. How much did one orange cost? How much did one apple cost?

In Chapter Two you learned how to solve one equation with one unknown and realized that an equation behaves like a balance in equilibrium, with the value of the left side equal to the value of the right side (see Fig.1). To answer the two questions of this problem, you are being asked to determine two values of two unknowns: the unit price x of one orange and the unit price y of one apple. Hence, the statement of the problem results in two equations:

$$10x + 10y = \$5.00 \tag{1}$$
$$5x + 12y = \$3.90. \tag{2}$$

Equations like (1) and (2) are called linear equations because their graphs in the Cartesian plane are straight lines (Chapter Seven, Section 2). They are called simultaneous linear equations because they must be solved at the same time.

Their solution is quite simple. It consists of eliminating x (or y) by making the number in front of the unknown, called the **coefficient** of x (or y), the same in both equations and then subtracting one equation from the other.

In our example, all we have to do is multiply the coefficients on both sides of the second equation by 2, so that the coefficient of x becomes 10 in both equations. We know we can do this because multiplying both sides of an equation by the same number leaves it in balance. Then we subtract the first equation from the resulting second equation, thereby eliminating x:

$$10x + 24y = \$7.80 \tag{3}$$
$$(-) \quad 10x + 10y = \$5.00 \tag{1}$$
$$\overline{\ 0 + 14y = \$2.80.}$$

Dividing both sides of the last equation by 14, we obtain $y = \$2.80/14 = \$0.20$. Now, substituting this value for y into equation (1):

$$10x + (10 \cdot \$0.20) = \$5.00,$$

we obtain:

$$10x = \$5.00 - (10 \cdot \$0.20) = \$3.00,$$

and, dividing both sides of this last equation by 10:

$$x = \$3.00/10 = \$0.30.$$

The solution is $x = \$0.30$ and $y = \$0.20$. You should check this by substituting these values into equations (1) and (2).

Math Camp 22

1 Solve the example in Section 1 by eliminating y first, then computing first x and then y.

2 Determine graphically (see Chapter Seven) the values of x and y that are solutions of the two simultaneous linear equations:

$$y = x; y = 3.$$

3 Determine graphically the values of x and y that are solutions of the two simultaneous linear equations:

$$3x - 24 = 12; -3x + y = 10.$$

Check your answers by substituting them into the two equations. Then find the solution algebraically by eliminating x first.

4 Determine graphically the values of x and y that are solutions of the two simultaneous linear equations:

$$12x + 4y = 16; 12x - 4y = 8.$$

Check your answers by substituting them into the two equations. Then find the solution algebraically by eliminating first either x or y.

5 You can buy one bottle of French wine and two bottles of California wine for $35 and two bottles of French wine and two of California wine for $50. What are the unit prices of the bottles of French and California wines?

6 You can buy two chocolate bars and one Coke for $1.00, or one chocolate bar and two Cokes for $1.25. How much does one chocolate bar cost? How much does one Coke cost?

7 In a money transaction during a trip in Europe, you bought 500 American dollars and 200 German marks for 1,200,000 Italian lire. In a second transaction, you bought 100 American dollars and 300 German marks for 760,000 Italian lire. How many lire did you get for 1 dollar and how many for 1 mark?

8 During a car trip, you bought 10 gallons of gas and 2 quarts of oil for $19.60 at one gas station, and then you bought 13 gallons of gas and 1 quart of oil for $20.20 at another gas station. Assuming the gas stations have the same prices, how much did 1 gallon of gas and 1 quart of oil cost?

9 The master masons who build the brick facade of a building are paid $9 an hour for an 8-hour day; apprentices are paid $5 an hour for an 8-hour day. Their combined wages amount to $2,040 a day. The same number of masons and apprentices building the brick facade of another building are paid respectively $10 an hour and $6 an hour for 8-hour days. Their combined salaries amount to $2,320 a day. How many masons and how many apprentices worked on each building?

10 A grocery store sells one make of coffee at $4.70 a pound and another for $2.70 a pound. How many pounds of each coffee should be mixed to sell the mixture at $3.70 a pound?

11 During a school raffle, 200 tickets were sold at $1.00 each to parents and at $0.50 each to students. The raffle collected $150.00. How many parents and how many students bought tickets?

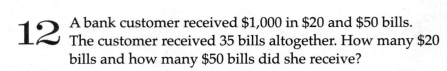

12 A bank customer received $1,000 in $20 and $50 bills. The customer received 35 bills altogether. How many $20 bills and how many $50 bills did she receive?

Chapter 9

Permutations and Combinations

 PERMUTATIONS AND COMBINATIONS

How many different three-digit numbers can be formed using the three digits 2, 5, 8 if digits cannot be repeated? The answer is six. The six numbers, in order of increasing size, are: 258, 285, 528, 582, 825, 852.

Mathematicians have chosen words and developed formulas to make it easier to answer questions like the one above. Different formulas are just shorthand notation for different situations. Once you understand the meaning of the words and formulas, you will be able to count faster. You will also discover that you can figure out the answers without memorizing the formulas, just by understanding the ideas behind the words. The best way to do this is to look at examples.

THE BIRTHDAY PARTY

Your father, your mother, and your sister wish to celebrate your birthday with a picnic in the park. As soon as they get there, your father takes your picture, which we will represent by the symbol:

(A),

where the letter A indicates you. But then your mother insists that she wants a picture of both her children. So your father takes two different pictures, which, indicating your sister by the letter B, we will represent as:

(AB), (BA),

meaning that in the first picture you appear on one side of your sister and in the second on her other side. But, as soon as Father has taken these two pictures, he begs Mother to join her two children and (representing Mother by the letter C) he takes six different pictures:

(ABC), (ACB), (CAB), (CBA), (BCA), (BAC).

Then a kind gentleman passing by offers to take pictures of the entire family and . . . he finds that he can take 24 different pictures!

I believe that you have already guessed how many different pictures can be taken with an increasing number of persons: 1 picture of one person, $1 \times 2 = 2$ pictures of two persons, $1 \times 2 \times 3 = 6$ pictures of three persons, $1 \times 2 \times 3 \times 4 = 24$ pictures of four persons, and so on.

In mathematics, the number of possible ways in which n objects can be arranged in a line is called the number of **linear permutations** of the n objects. (The word "permutation" comes from the Latin "permutare," meaning "to exchange.") The number of possible linear permutations is the product of all the integers from 1 to n:

$$1 \times 2 \times 3 \times \ldots \times (n-2) \times (n-1) \times n = n! \qquad (1)$$

a product symbolized by $n!$ and called *n factorial*. The exclamation point after the n is more than justified, because as n becomes larger and larger, n factorial grows tremendously fast. If you had two sisters instead of one, the pictures of your family, now containing five people, could be taken in $5! = 5 \times 4 \times 3 \times 2 \times 1 = 120$ different ways. It is said that a picture of 10 members of the United Nations could take 10 years to shoot (even if 1,000 pictures were taken each day) if, for "diplomatic reasons," the 10 U.N. members wanted the picture taken in all possible positions. This would lead to 10! or 3,628,800 positions.

🎲 THE PIZZA SHOP

When eating lunch in a pizza shop, you and three friends sit at a circular table with four chairs. How many different ways can the four of you sit around the table?

Starting with you, it is possible for any one of three friends to sit on your right side, either of two remaining friends to sit on the right side of that friend, and the remaining one friend then sits in the last chair, on your left side. The number of possible arrangements around the table is the product of these possibilities: $3 \times 2 \times 1 = 6$. We illustrate these six different sitting arrangements below; the letter A indicates you and the other letters indicate your friends.

$$\begin{pmatrix} D & C \\ A & B \end{pmatrix}\begin{pmatrix} C & D \\ A & B \end{pmatrix}\begin{pmatrix} D & B \\ A & C \end{pmatrix}\begin{pmatrix} B & D \\ A & C \end{pmatrix}\begin{pmatrix} C & B \\ A & D \end{pmatrix}\begin{pmatrix} B & C \\ A & D \end{pmatrix}$$

You will find the same number of possible sitting arrangements, six, if you count by going to your left instead of to your right, or if you start counting from any other person at the table. (Try it.)

One day, a fourth friend joins you for lunch. Now what is the number of different ways that you and your four friends can sit around the table?

It is now possible for any one of four friends to sit to your right, any of three remaining friends to sit to the right of that friend, either of two remaining friends to sit to the right of that friend, and the remaining one friend then sits to your left. Now the number of different possible arrangements is $4 \times 3 \times 2 \times 1 = 24$.

These are examples of what mathematicians call **circular permutations,** whereas Section 2 considered linear permutations. You should notice that the number of ways of arranging n different items in a line is $n!$, whereas the number of ways of arranging n different items in a circle is $(n-1)!$.

Perhaps now is a good time to point out that we have been using a simple counting rule that mathematicians call the **multiplication principle.** A simple way to state it is:

If there are P possibilities, each of which can then be followed by Q other possibilities, then altogether there are $P \times Q$ possibilities.

You can do some fast counting just by using this idea over and over again. For example, in a line of four people, one place in line may be filled by any of four possibilities. Once that place is filled, the second place may be filled by any of three remaining possibilities. So far, the multiplication principle says that there are 4×3 possibilities. Once two people are in line, the third place may be filled by any of two remaining possibilities. Now the multiplication principle says there are $(4 \times 3) \times 2$ possibilities. Once three people are in line, the last place must be filled by the one remaining person. So the multiplication principle says that altogether there are $((4 \times 3) \times 2) \times 1 = 4! = 24$ ways that four people can stand in line.

🎲 REPEATING YOURSELF

Let's go back to our earlier question but change the way we look at it. How many different three-digit numbers can be formed using the three digits 2, 5, 8 if no digits can be repeated? Try thinking as follows: "This is like taking all possible pictures of three different people. The 2 might be me, the 5 might be Mother, and the 8 might be Father. This is the same as a linear permutation of three objects, so I know the answer is $3 \times 2 \times 1 = 3! = 6$."

But what happens if the digits can be repeated? This cannot be a simple linear permutation because you cannot repeat yourself. The number 225 is not a possible photograph, unless trick photography is being used.

Knowing repetitions are allowed, you can now count as follows. It is possible for the first digit to be any one of the three digits; the second digit can also be any one of the three; and the third digit can be any of the three. The answer is $3 \times 3 \times 3 = 3^3 = 27$.

Try writing these 27 different numbers down, putting them in ascending numerical order. But first try picturing them as follows. Six have no repeated digits, and from Section 1 we know these are 258, 285, 528, 582, 825, 852. Three more, having only repeated digits, are 222, 555, 888. The other 18 have exactly two identical digits, like 225, which is the smallest one of these 18 numbers. I suggest you write the remaining 17 down. Then you can easily put all 27 in ascending order.

How many different four-digit numbers with repetitions can be formed from the digits 2, 4, 5, 9? Before reading the next paragraph, you should reread the previous paragraph and then write down your answer.

If you got the answer $4 \times 4 \times 4 \times 4 = 4^4 = 64$, you are right! Now I can tell you about some useful counting formulas by using the words chosen by mathematicians.

🎲 USING THE WORDS OF MATHEMATICIANS

You now know how to count "the number of linear permutations of n different objects, without repetitions" (as in a photograph). And you can do it quickly! It is $n!$.

And you can figure out the "number of linear permutations of n different objects, with repetitions." It is n^n.

At this point, a curious mathematician might ask, "Which is larger, $n!$ or n^n?" If you think about how we got these two formulas, you suspect (and then realize) that n^n must be larger than $n!$

because of repetitions. Try a few values of n and you will find this is true as long as n is not 1. When $n = 1$, there is just one object and there is only one way to place that object. Since, as you know, $1^1 = 1$, the formula n^n makes sense for $n = 1$. But the answer from both formulas should be the same when $n = 1$, so mathematicians have decided that 1! must equal 1. That is, 1! = 1. So if you ask, "Does $n!$ have a value when n is 1?", a mathematician will say, "Yes, it is equal to 1." Mathematicians even define zero factorial as 1 with the expression 0! = 1, simply because it makes their counting formulas more convenient.

In mathematics, a "permutation of n things taken r at a time with repetitions" means the following. Think of r positions in a line (like a number with r digits). Any one of n different things can go in the first position. Since repetitions are allowed, any one of n things can go in the second position. Then any of n things can go in the third position. Continuing in this way until all r positions have been filled, the total number of possibilities is the product of n with itself r times or, in exponential notation, n^r.

A mathematician would therefore say: "The number of permutations of n things taken r at a time with repetitions is equal to n^r." It is understood that the n items are distinct (different from one another). If the n items were the same, how could you recognize and count different arrangements?

Now you can quickly answer the question, "How many ways can the letters A, C, E be arranged, two at a time, if letters may be repeated?" This is the same as "permuting three things two at a time with repetitions," or $3^2 = 9$. (The nine possibilities are: AA, AC, AE, CA, CC, CE, EA, EC, EE.)

You are now able to count even faster. For example, what if you want to know, "How many ways can the letters of the alphabet be arranged three at a time when repetitions are allowed?" You can now figure out that the answer is: $26 \times 26 \times 26 = 26^3 = 17,576$. (Of course, many of these combinations of three letters are not going to spell words.)

What if you want to know, "How many ways can the letters of the alphabet be arranged three at a time without repetitions?" I am sure you can now figure out the answer to be: $26 \times 25 \times 24 = 15,600$.

The number of "permutations of n things taken r at a time without repetitions" is symbolized by $P(n,r)$. The words and the symbol are both shorthand for "the number of ways that r items can be selected, without repetitions, from n (distinct) items and put in a line with r positions, where all possible ordered arrangements of the *r* items are counted." This is a mouthful, which is why mathematicians prefer a formula.

Let's count $P(n,r)$ as follows. Any one of *n* items can go in the first position. Since repetitions are not allowed, any one of the $(n-1)$ remaining items can go in the second position. Then any one of $(n-2)$ remaining items can go in the third position. This continues until any one of the $(n-r+1)$ remaining items goes in the last position. So the total number of possible arrangements is:

$$P(n,r) = n \times (n-1) \times (n-2) \times \ldots \times (n-r+1).$$

In factorial notation, this is the same as:

$$P(n,r) = \frac{n!}{(n-r)!} \tag{2}$$

because:

$$\frac{n!}{(n-r)!} = \frac{n \times (n-1) \times (n-2)\ldots(n-r+1)}{1} \times \frac{(n-r) \times (n-r-1)\ldots \times 2 \times 1}{(n-r) \times (n-r-1)\ldots \times 2 \times 1}.$$

Summarizing in words and symbols: The number of (linear) permutations of *n* (distinct) things taken *r* at a time is equal to n^r if repetitions are allowed, but it is equal to $P(n,r)$ if repetitions are not allowed.

So let's calculate the number of permutations of 26 things taken three at a time without repetitions: $P(26,3) = 26!/23! = 26 \times 25 \times 24 = 15,600$. This is the same as the number of ways that the letters of the alphabet can be arranged three at a time without repetitions. Some people prefer to use the formula, equation (2), and some people prefer to use the multiplication principle, given just above it, but the answer is the same.

🎲 THE U.S. ALPINE CLUB

The U.S. Alpine Club is a group of passionate mountain climbers who exercise their skills by climbing walls every Sunday. They climb in teams of two, often exchanging positions as leader and second. Among them is one group of six students, whom we will label 1, 2, 3, 4, 5, 6, who exercise on some walls not far from New York City. They exchange lead positions and consider a team like (2,3) with 2 as its leader to be different from the team (3,2) with 3 as its leader. How many different teams of two climbers can they put together?

The different teams may be represented by the two inverted pyramids shown below. The second pyramid was obtained from the first one by interchanging the leader with the second position in each team of the first pyramid:

$$(1,2); (1,3); (1,4); (1,5); (1,6);$$
$$(2,3); (2,4); (2,5); (2,6);$$
$$(3,4); (3,5); (3,6);$$
$$(4,5); (4,6);$$
$$(5,6).$$

$$(2,1); (3,1); (4,1); (5,1); (6;1);$$
$$(3,2); (4,2); (5,2); (6,2);$$
$$(4,3); (4,2); (4,1);$$
$$(5,4); (6,4);$$
$$(6,5).$$

By counting the number of teams in one of the pyramids and then doubling that number, we find the number of possible teams to be:

$$2 \times (5 + 4 + 3 + 2 + 1) = 2 \times 15 = 30.$$

A faster way to count is to realize that the first team member (the leader) can be any of six different students and the other member can be any one of the remaining five. So the number of possible teams is: $6 \times 5 = 30$. Or, if you prefer the formula (2), the number of teams equals the number of "permutations of 6 students taken 2 at a time":

$$P(6,2) = 6! / (6 - 2)! = (6 \times 5 \times 4 \times 3 \times 2 \times 1) / (4 \times 3 \times 2 \times 1) = 30.$$

On the other hand, if the climbers do not consider leaders to be different from those in the second position—for example, if they consider (2,3) to be the same as (3,2), the number of teams is obviously one-half the number of the previous count, or 15 teams. This sort of counting, which ignores the order of the team members, is called the **combination** of n items taken r at a time, symbolized by $C(n,r)$. It can be calculated with the following formula:

$$C(n,r) = n! / (r! \times (n - r)!) \tag{3}$$

With $n = 6$ and $r = 2$, equation (3) gives:

$$6! / (2! \times 4!) = (6 \times 5 \times 4 \times 3 \times 2 \times 1)/(2 \times 1 \times 4 \times 3 \times 2 \times 1)$$
$$= 720 / 48 = 15.$$

7 THE GRADUATION PROM

Three girls (1,2,3) and three boys (4,5,6) graduating the same day from the same high school go to the graduation prom together. How many couples could be formed during the evening of the prom?

If the couples are all "going steady," then there would be three steady couples, say (1,4), (2,5), and (3,6). But if the couples were not going steady, any of the three boys could dance with any of the three girls, and there would be $3 \times 3 = 9$ different couples. (Of course only three couples could actually dance at the same time.)

Finally, and in fun, if boys could also dance with boys and girls with girls, there would be as many "couples" as in the examples of the mountain-climbing teams (Section 6). That is, there would be either 15 or 30 couples, depending on your assumptions. If you assume that couples with the same pair of numbers, such as (2,5) and (5,2), are the same, the answer would be 15. If all possible couples are viewed as different (because, for example, one person leads while the other follows during a dance), there would be 30 couples.

8 SITTING IN CLASS

Now that you have become familiar with n factorial, you might be interested to investigate in how many ways you and your classmates can sit in class.

If your class consists of n students and there are n chairs in the room facing the blackboard, you already know that the linear permutation of n positions is $n!$. Even for a class of only 25 students, the number of permutations becomes enormous, because 25! is more than 10^{25}. (To three figures of accuracy, $25! = 1.55 \times 10^{25}$.)

Let us now assume that there is one extra chair in the classroom. In how many ways can the n students sit in the $n + 1$ chairs?

As you are aware, there are often several ways of thinking about a problem and then solving it. In a counting problem like this, the result should be the same no matter how we look at it. Let's look at three solutions.

Solution I. There are $n!$ ways that the n students can seat themselves in n chairs while leaving chair 1 empty. Similarly, there are another $n!$ ways with chair 2 empty. And there are another $n!$

ways with chair 3 empty, and so forth, until the last chair, $n + 1$, is left empty. So we need to add $n!$ to itself, over and over, $n + 1$ times. This is the same as $(n + 1) \times n! = (n + 1)!$

SOLUTION 2. A faster solution comes from using a cute trick. Imagine a "ghost" student sitting in the empty chair. Now you can see immediately that there are n students plus 1 ghost student, or $n + 1$ students. So the problem looks just like the permutation of $n + 1$ things, and the answer is $(n + 1)!$

SOLUTION 3. Here is another trick. Let's call this a game of musical chairs, but instead of letting the students choose the chairs on which they sit, let the chairs "choose" the students who sit in them. In other words, picture the students as staying still while the $n + 1$ chairs run around, taking a different student each time. Again, the solution is the number of permutations of $n + 1$ things (the chairs) taken n at a time (by the students), or, from equation (2):

$$P(n+1,n) = \frac{(n+1)!}{(n+1-n)!} = \frac{(n+1)!}{1!} = (n+1)!,$$

where now we have used $1! = 1$.

All three ways of looking at the problem give the same answer. Now, what happens if we have n students and r extra chairs?

If we use the idea in the third solution, we picture $n + r$ chairs playing musical chairs, and we know the answer is the number of permutations of $n + r$ things (the chairs) taken n at a time (by the students) or:

$$P(n + r,n) = (n + r)! / (n + r - n)! = (n + r)! / r!$$

If we use the idea of the second solution, we think of n students and r "ghost" students (in the empty chairs). If the ghosts were people (distinguishable) there would be $(n + r)!$ possible seatings. But because we cannot tell one ghost from another, we have already counted all possible orderings of these r ghosts in $(n + r)!$, which means that $(n + r)!$ accounts for $r!$ times more possibilities than it should. So divide by $r!$ and get the answer, $(n + r)! / r!$.

Regardless of how you look at it, if there are six students and eight chairs in the classroom, the number of permutations of eight chairs taken by six students at a time is:

$$P(8,6) = 8! / (8 - 6)! = (8 \times 7 \times 6 \times 5 \times 4 \times 3 \times 2 \times 1) / (2 \times 1) = 20,160$$

What a large number of possibilities for such a small number of chairs and students! I bet you did not expect it.

Math Camp 23

1 Five friends have their photographs taken on commencement day. If they take the photographs in groups of three, how many different photographs can they end up taking?

2 In how many ways can four people sit around a square table that seats four diners?

3 The American tennis team for the Davis Cup consists of four players chosen from among a group of 10 aspiring players. How many groups of four players are possible?

4 Five ladies and five gentlemen participate in a tennis competition to choose two players for a mixed doubles tournament. How many player combinations can participate in the trials?

5 The following five-course menu is offered at a banquet:

Course	Choose one
1	**Italian Salad** *or* **Melon.**
2	**Spaghetti with Tomato Sauce** *or* **Minestrone Soup.**
3	**Veal Cutlet** *or* **Sole Meuniére.**
4	**Chocolate Ice Cream** *or* **Fresh Fruit.**
5	**Coffee** *or* **Tea.**

How many different dinners can be chosen from the menu, assuming that each diner chooses one item for each course of the menu?

6 The compartment of a European train consists of two facing rows of four seats each. In how many ways can eight travelers sit in the compartment? In how many ways can six travelers sit in the compartment?

7 Jane goes to buy two pairs of shoes. She is shown 10 pairs that fit her. In how many ways can she choose two pairs of shoes?

8 A painter must decide how to exhibit six of his paintings at an exhibition. How many choices does he have if the paintings must be shown in a horizontal row?

9 A librarian has nine books that are to be displayed on a desk in three groups of three, ignoring their titles. In how many different ways can the books be placed on the desk?

10 You have six pairs of gray socks in your dresser drawer. In how many ways can you choose a pair of gray socks (even if the grays are not quite identical)?

11 You have five best friends at school. In how many ways can you invite two of them to your birthday party?

Chapter 10

The Mathematics of Chance

 **THROWING PENNIES**

Pennies and other U.S. coins have the head of one or another famous American on one side and some symbol of our country, like the bald eagle on quarters, on the other. The sides are called "heads," for the head side, and "tails" for the other side. For our purposes, we will call the sides H and T.

When we throw a penny it may land either H up and T down, or H down and T up. In other words, it is certain that it will come down either one way or the other. (If we cannot decide which side is up, because for example the penny is leaning against a wall, we disregard the throw and try again.)

The mathematical theory of probability is the fascinating study of chance happenings. It provides answers to questions like "What is the chance that a thrown penny will land H up?" However, it cannot answer questions like "Will this penny land H up on the next throw?" or "How many more throws until this penny lands H up?" There are many important problems for which we cannot compute exactly when something will happen, but we can compute the chance, called the **probability,** that it will happen if circumstances repeat over and over again.

Probability theory assumes that the penny is "honest"; that is, has the same chance of falling H as falling T each time it is thrown. Under this assumption, we say that H and T have the same chance, or probability, p, of occurring for each throw, and assign to p the value $1/2$, so that the sum of the two probabilities adds up to 1, which is called **certainty** ($1/2 + 1/2 = 1$).

An honest penny is also assumed to have an independent chance of falling H or T every time it is thrown, meaning that a thrown penny is not influenced by the preceding throws. Thus, whatever the Hs or Ts of the preceding throws, the next throw has the same probability, 1/2, of falling H or T. From now on, we shall assume that all of our pennies are honest.

Let us now ask what can happen if we throw the same penny twice. The following four possible sequences of Hs and Ts may occur:

$$HH, HT, TH, \text{ or } TT,$$

and since the throws are independent of each other, each of these four combinations has a chance of 1 out of 4, or 1/4, which is equal to the product of the chance 1/2 of each of the two separate throws; that is, $1/2 \times 1/2 = 1/4$. The sum of these four probabilities is 1, which is certainty, and there are no other possibilities.

Now we may ask: "What is the chance of getting two Hs (or two Ts) in a row?" We know that the chance of an H in the first throw is 1/2, and the independent chance in the second throw is also 1/2. Therefore, the chance of two consecutive Hs (or two consecutive Ts) is $1/2 \times 1/2 = 1/4$. Similarly, the chance of getting H in five consecutive throws is:

$$1/2 \times 1/2 \times 1/2 \times 1/2 \times 1/2 = (1/2)^5 = 1/2^5 = 1/32 = 0.03125 \approx 0.03.$$

So the chance of getting five Hs (or five Ts) in a row is 1 in 32 throws, or about 3 in 100 throws (3%).

The chance of getting 10 Hs (or 10 Ts) in a row, as you might expect, is quite small:

$$(1/2)^{10} = 1/2^{10} = 1/(1{,}024) = 0.000976,$$

which is near 0.001, or about 1 in 1,000 throws!

Now, after getting 10 Hs in a row, you might ask: "What is the chance of the next throw being H?" Since your first 10 throws have no influence whatsoever on the next one, you should realize that throw 11 has 1/2 chance of being one more H as well as 1/2 chance to be the first T. The result of this kind of sequence of throws is expressed by the fundamental law of probability theory, which, for coin throws, is: "As the number N of independent coin throws increases, the ratio of the number of Hs to the number N asymptotically approaches the theoretical probability, $p = 1/2$," where the words "asymptotically approaches 1/2" mean "gets nearer and nearer 1/2 as N increases." Of course, the same can be said about Ts instead of Hs.

Table 7 illustrates the basic probability law for a series of 60 penny throws. For ease of reading, the series of Hs and Ts is arranged in 10 groups of six throws per group.

Table 7   A Series of 60 Penny Throws

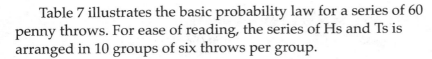

H,T,T,H,H,H;   T,T,H,T,H,T;   T,T,H,H,T,T;   H,T,T,H,T,T;   H,T,H,T,H,H;

T,H,T,T,H,H;   T,H,T,H,H,T;   T,H,H,T,H,H;   T,H,T,H,H,T;   T,T,H,H,H,T

Throw Number = N	1	2	3	4	5	...	57	58	59	60
Sum of Hs = h	1	1	1	2	3	...	28	29	30	30
h/N	1.00	0.50	0.33	0.50	0.60	...	0.49	0.50	0.51	0.50
t/N	0.00	0.50	0.67	0.50	0.40	...	0.51	0.50	0.49	0.50
Sum of Ts = t	0	1	2	2	2	...	29	29	29	30

The first row of Table 7, below the Hs and Ts, gives the throw number, N, for the first five throws and last four throws. (If the entire table were filled in, it would be several pages wide since it would have 60 columns, one for each throw.) The next row gives the number of Hs, called h, after each throw. The next row gives the ratio h/N. The last two rows show the corresponding numbers for the Ts. Notice that, for each throw, the two ratios h/N and t/N must add up to certainty = 1. Also notice that, as the number of throws increases, the ratio h/N asymptotically approaches the theoretical probability, $1/2 = 0.50$, in accord with the fundamental law of probability, and t/N also approaches $1/2$. Fig. 68 illustrates this asymptotic behavior by using Descartes's method of graphing data (Chapter Seven).

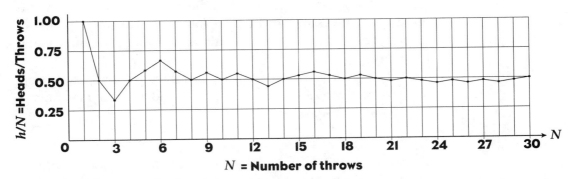

Figure 68 As the number of throws increases, the ratio of the number of heads to the number of throws asymptotically approaches $1/2 = 0.50$. (Data are the first 30 throws of Table 7.)

◆ PLAYING LOTTO

In the lotto of a casino, 50 balls numbered 1 to 50 are put into an urn. Six balls are taken out of the urn, one at a time, and the number of each ball is recorded. Each ball is put back into the urn before the next one is taken out. To hit the jackpot, you must guess all six recorded numbers. (Notice that the same number may appear more than once in this lotto.) What is your chance of hitting the jackpot?

Since the extracted balls are put back in the urn, there are always 50 balls in the urn. The probability of the first extracted ball's number matching any of your six guessed numbers is therefore 6 out of 50, or 6/50. The probability of the second extracted ball matching any of your five remaining guessed numbers is 5 out of 50, or 5/50. Similarly, the probability of the third extracted ball matching any of your four remaining guessed numbers is 4/50, then 3/50, 2/50, and 1/50.

To hit the jackpot, you must have guessed all six extracted numbers; that is, you must have simultaneously gotten all six probabilities, and your jackpot probability is the product of your six single probabilities:

$$(6/50) \times (5/50) \times (4/50) \times (3/50) \times (2/50) \times (1/50) =$$
$$(6 \times 5 \times 4 \times 3 \times 2 \times 1)/50^6 = 720/15,625,000,000 = 0.00000004608$$

or 1 in 1/0.00000004608; that is, 1 time in 21,701,389 bets! Clearly, it does not pay to bet on such a lotto.

◆ THE CAR LICENSE-PLATE GAME

When you sit next to the driver of a car during a long, slow, boring trip, I suggest you play this game. It will show you how different and interesting the license plate of the car traveling in front of you can be, as well as a different application of probability theory.

Let us say a "standard" car plate consists of three numbers on the left and three letters on the right. A standard plate may be represented by the sequence:

$$N_1 N_2 N_3 - L_1 L_2 L_3.$$

Since each of the three plate numbers can be chosen from among the 10 numbers 0 to 9 (yes, there are plates with the number 000), the possible combinations of three numbers are $10 \times 10 \times 10 = 10^3$; that is, all the combinations of three numbers on a license plate are 1,000.

Similarly, since the letters of the English alphabet are 26, all the combinations of three letters on a license plate are $26^3 =$ 17,516, and all the possible standard plates are:

$$1,000 \times 17,516 = 17,516,000.$$

CHALLENGE 1. How many license plates can have three different numbers?

You can choose the first of the three numbers in 10 different ways from the numbers 0 to 9. The second number can only be chosen from the nine remaining numbers, and the third from the eight remaining numbers. So three different numbers can be chosen in $10 \times 9 \times 8 = 720$ ways out of the $10 \times 10 \times 10 = 1,000$ ways each separate number can be chosen.

The probability p_d of a car plate having three different numbers is thus:

$$p_d = 720/1,000 = 0.72,$$

or almost 3 in 4.

CHALLENGE 2. How many license plates do not have all different numbers?

Since the probability p_d of all three numbers being different plus the probability p_s of their not being all different add up to a certainty (that is, to a probability of 1) the probability p_s that all three numbers be not equal is:

$$p_s = 1 - p_d = 1 - 0.72 = 0.28,$$

or slightly more than 1 in 4.

CHALLENGE 3. How many license plates have three different letters?

You may choose the first letter in 26 ways among the 26 letters of the English alphabet, the second in 25 ways among the remaining 25 letters, and the third in 24 ways among the remaining 24 letters, resulting in a total of:

$$26 \times 25 \times 24 = 15,600 \text{ ways.}$$

Hence, there are 15,600 license plates with different letters among the $26 \times 26 \times 26 = 17,576$ standard plates, yielding a probability of $15,600/17,576 = 0.887$. (The probability of license plates with three letters that are not different is $1 - 0.887 = 0.113$.)

I leave it to you to determine many more license-plate probabilities in Math Camp 24 at the end of this chapter. Have a good time while sitting next to your driver!

SHOOTING CRAPS (THE SIMPLE WAY)

A simplified game of craps consists of throwing two cubic dice, each of which has 1 to 6 dots on its six faces. Two players try to guess the sum of the dots appearing on the top two faces of the dice. The player guessing the number nearest the sum of the dots is the winner.

For example, if player A guesses 7 and player B guesses 9 and the top dots are 4 and 6, adding up to 10, then B wins because 9 is nearer to 10 than 7.

Let's find the probabilities associated with the two players of this simplified craps game. We will use the fact that the probability of a specific event in a sequence of events is equal to the ratio of the number of times the specific event may occur to the number of all possible events.

CHALLENGE 4. What is the probability that a specific number of dots, say 3 dots, will appear on the top face of one die?

Since any of the six faces of a die may appear as the top face, any of 1, 2, 3, 4, 5, or 6 dots may appear on the top face of the die. There are six equally likely outcomes possible (assuming honest dice). Only one of these six outcomes matches the specified outcome. Thus, 3 dots has 1 chance out of 6 or 1/6 of appearing on the top face of the die.

CHALLENGE 5. What is the probability of two specific numbers of dots, say 2 and 5, appearing as the top faces of two dice, A and B?

The probability of 2 dots on the top face of die A is 1 out of 6; the probability of 5 dots on the top face of die B is also 1 out of 6. For the two events to occur simultaneously, their probabilities have to be multiplied. Hence, the probability of this particular event is $(1/6) \times (1/6) = 1/36$ or 1 in 36 throws.

If we ask the same question but allow 2 and 5 to appear on the top faces of either die, the event can happen in two ways, with 2 on die A and 5 on die B, or with 2 on die B and 5 on die A. Hence, the required probability becomes $2 \times (1/36) = 1/18$, or 1 in 18 throws.

CHALLENGE 6. What is the probability that the sum of the dots on the top faces of dice A and B add up to 10?

The sum of two numbers between 1 and 6 adds up to 10 in only two ways: $4 + 6 = 10$ and $5 + 5 = 10$. Hence, the number of

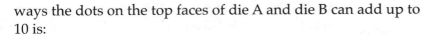

ways the dots on the top faces of die A and die B can add up to 10 is:

> 4 on A and 6 on B;
>
> 5 on A and 5 on B;
>
> 6 on A and 4 on B;

or in three ways. The six faces of die A and the six faces of die B can appear in $6 \times 6 = 36$ ways. Hence, the probability that the dots on the top faces of A and B add to 10 is $3/36 = 1/12$, or 1 in 12 throws.

CHALLENGE 7. Which of the two players had a better chance of winning?

Remember that Player A chose 7 and Player B chose 9. Player A wins whenever the dots on top add up to 7 or less. Player B wins whenever the dots on top add up to 9 or higher. There is a tie whenever the dots add up to 8.

Assuming honest dice, there are six equally likely ways that die A can land and, for each of these, there are six equally likely ways that die B can land. This makes a total of $6 \times 6 = 36$ ways that the two dice can land. Let's list these 36 possible outcomes (or events), grouping them by total dots on the tops of the dice, as shown in Table 8.

Table 8

Total on Dice	Die A + Die B	Number of Ways
2	1+1	1
3	1+2, 2+1	2
4	1+3, 2+2, 3+1	3
5	1+4, 2+3, 3+2, 4+1	4
6	1+5, 2+4, 3+3, 4+2, 5+1	5
7	1+6, 2+5, 3+4, 4+3, 5+2, 6+1	6
8	2+6, 3+5, 4+4, 5+3, 6+2	5
9	3+6, 4+5, 5+4, 6+3	4
10	4+6, 5+5, 6+4	3
11	5+6, 6+5	2
12	6+6	1

As you can see, the number of equally likely ways where the dice total 7 or less is $1 + 2 + 3 + 4 + 5 + 6 = 21$ ways. There are $1 + 2 + 3 + 4 = 10$ ways where the dice total 9 or more, and there are 5 ways where the dice total 8. There are no other possibilities. So there are 21 ways for Player A to win, 10 ways for Player B to win, and 5 ways they can tie. Clearly Player A has a better chance of winning. In fact, Player A is more than twice as likely to win.

There are 21 ways for Player A to win, 10 ways for Player B to win, and 5 ways they can tie. Each of these has the same chance of happening (is equally likely), and there are no other possibilities. The number of ways 2 dice can fall is $6 \times 6 = 36$. The probability of Player A winning is $21/36 = 0.58333\ldots$, or about 58% of all throws; the probability of Player B winning is $10/36 = 0.2777\ldots$, or about 28% of all throws; and the probability of a tie is $5/36 = 0.13888\ldots$, or about 14% of all throws. The sum is 1.00, or 100% of all throws where a player can win, lose, or tie.

———— Math 🎋 Camp ————
24

1 Throw a penny 10, 20, and 50 times in a row and compute the ratio h/N after each series of throws as in Table 7. Does it approach $1/2$? To solve this problem in less time, throw 10, 20, and 50 ($= 80$) pennies at the same time and compare the value of the ratio h/N after the three throws with that of a single throw of 80 pennies.

2 Repeat the experiment in problem 1 with any other type of coin (nickel, dime, quarter, or half-dollar, if you can get that many).

3 What are the probabilities of getting sequences of 5 Hs, 10 Hs, and 20 Hs in a row? What is the probability of getting 1 more H after each of the preceding sequences?

4 What is the probability of getting 5 Ts in a row followed by 5 Hs in a row? What is the probability of an H after the sequence of 5 Ts and of 5 Hs in a row?

5 What is the probability of guessing the first and the third number in the lotto of this chapter's Section 2? What is the probability of guessing the first two numbers?

6 A 50-ball lotto does not throw back the first six balls in the urn. What is the probability of hitting the jackpot?

7 A lotto uses only 10 balls in the urn and throws each extracted ball into the urn before extracting the next one. It gives the jackpot to the player who guesses the numbers of the first two extracted balls. What is the probability of hitting the jackpot?

8 The chance of a penny falling tails up is $1/2$ and the chance of a die falling with 5 dots on its upper face is $1/6$. What is the chance of these two events occurring simultaneously? (The chance of two different events occurring simultaneously is the product of their separate chances.)

9 You feel that your chance of winning a tennis tournament in May is $9/10$ and that your chance of winning a tournament in June is $8/10$. What do you believe the chance of your winning both tournaments to be?

10 What is the probability of a standard car plate (see Section 3 of this chapter) having three equal numbers?

11 What is the probability of a standard car plate having three equal letters?

12 What is the probability of a standard car plate having all different numbers and all different letters?

13 What is the probability of a standard car plate having all equal numbers and all equal letters?

14 What is the probability of shooting two 1s in a simplified game of craps?

15 What is the probability of shooting two even numbers in a simplified game of craps?

16 What is the probability of shooting two equal numbers in a simplified game of craps?

Math Camp

1 350;   4,925;   1,200,345

2 Four hundred twenty-one, point twenty-five;

Forty-two thousand, three hundred seventy-five, point three seventy-four;

Twenty-one billion, three hundred million, seven hundred fifty thousand, two hundred twenty-one, point zero forty-five.

3 $3 \times 10^2 + 2 \times 10^1 + 1 \times 10^0$

$2 \times 10^5 + 5 \times 10^4 + 4 \times 10^3 + 3 \times 10^2 + 2 \times 10^1 + 1 \times 10^0 + 4 \times 10^{-1} + 5 \times 10^{-2} + 6 \times 10^{-3}$

$5 \times 10^{11} + 0 \times 10^{10} + 0 \times 10^9 + 4 \times 10^8 + 0 \times 10^7 + 1 \times 10^6 + 3 \times 10^5 + 0 \times 10^4 + 2 \times 10^3 + 0 \times 10^2 + 0 \times 10^1 + 2 \times 10^0$

4 5,034;   6,050,200,000;   30,205

5 234.35;   0.456;   12,000.46

answers

1
$$21_{10} = 10101_2 \, ;$$
$$248.625_{10} = 11111000.101_2 \, ;$$
$$2{,}003{,}481_{10} = 11101001001000011001_2 \, ;$$
$$0.3125_{10} = 0.0101_2 \, .$$

2
$$1010_2 = 10_{10} \, ;$$
$$11001_2 = 25_{10} \, ;$$
$$1100_2 + 011_2 = 12_{10} + 3_{10} = 15_{10} \, ;$$
$$1010_2 + 101_2 - 10_2 = 10_{10} + 5_{10} - 2_{10} = 13_{10} \, ;$$
$$111_2 + 1010_2 - 11_2 = 7_{10} + 10_{10} - 3_{10} = 14_{10} \, ;$$
$$1001_2 \times 110_2 = 9_{10} \times 6_{10} = 54_{10} \, .$$

———— Math Camp ————
3

1 716; 3,622; 10,006,249; $12.85; 368,353 mi.

2 $11.27

3 $6.59

4 26 mi.

5 9,350 mi.

6 $26,545.15

Math Camp 4

1 The parents spent $20 each on gifts for John, his 4 married brothers and 3 married sisters, and the 7 spouses, or $(1 + 4 + 3 + 7) \times \$20 = \$300$. They spent $15 each on John's 6 unmarried cousins, or $6 \times \$15 = \$90$. John's parents spent $\$300 + \$90 = \$390$ on Christmas gifts.

2 The river begins at 3 mph, then flows at $2 \times 3 = 6$ mph, and finally, during the last 10 mi., flows at $3 \times 6 = 18$ mph.

3 The first soccer player gets the ball at 25 mph and passes it at $2 \times 25 = 50$ mph to the second player, who kicks it into the goal at $1.5 \times 50 = 75$ mph.

Math Camp 5

1 $\$3,429 - \$1,307 = \$2,122$ is left in the account.

2 $\$5,000 - \$1,409 - \$517 - \$2,098 = \$976$ is left in the account.

3 $95°F - 48°F = 47°F$. The temperature decreased 47°F.

4 If the students do not know already, they should do some research to find out where Albany, Washington, D.C., and New York City are located in relation to each other. The distance between Albany and New York City is 470 mi. – 220 mi. = 250 mi.

5 $900 - 12 - 15 - 21 = 852$ students attended school.

6 George Washington was $1799 - 1732 = 67$ years old when he died.

7 The groceries cost $\$10.75 + \$4.50 + \$6.52 + \$2.25 = \$24.02$. So change from the $50.00 bill should be $\$50.00 - \$24.02 = \$25.98$.

Math Camp

6

1 The manufacturer makes a profit of $4,550 \times 10\% = \$455$, so the dealer pays $\$4,550 + \$455 = \$5,005$. The dealer makes a profit of $\$5,005 \times 20\% = \$1,001$, so the customer pays $\$5,005 + \$1,001 = \$6,006$.

2 The second-place winner drove at $(100 + 100 \times 10\%)$ mph = 110 mph. The winner drove at $(110 + 110 \times 20\%)$ mph = 132 mph.

3 The average height of one floor is $1,300 / 110 = 12$ ft., to the nearest foot.

4 The floor height is 9 feet, which is $9 \times 12 = 108$ in. One step is 9 inches high, so $108/9 = 12$ steps are needed to go from one floor to the next.

5 200 ft. $\times$ 200 ft. = 40,000 sq. ft.; $520,000/40,000 = 13$ lots.

6 2 hrs. 10 min. = 130 min. so the average speed is $130/26.2 = 5$ min./mi. (mile after mile, for over 26 mi.).

7 The plane's average speed is $4,500/8 = 562.5$ mph between the two cities.

8 Each employee wins $\$22,500,000/75 = \$300,000$.

9 The cost is $\$2,115,000/(900 \text{ sq. ft.}) = \$2,350/\text{sq. ft.}$

10 15 ft. equals $15 \times 12 = 180$ in., so there are $180/0.125 = 1,440$ ants in line, assuming no separation between ants.

11 The price is $\$5.97/3 = \$1.99$ per pint.

12 The wholesaler sells the 397 dresses at $200 per dress, or $79,400. He makes a profit of $\$79,400 - \$59,550 = \$19,850$ on this transaction.

13 $531,245 > 521,245$; $618,100,223 > 618,000,222$; $422,112 > 422,111$.

14 234.87 < 243.92;   0.0963 < 0.5742;
123,675,234 < 123,765,234.

15 After 6 months, Jack's bank account of $100 has grown 5%, or $100 × 5/100 = $100 × 0.05 = $5, so he has $100 + $5 = $105. After another 6 months (1 year), his $105 has grown by $105.00 × 0.05 = $5.25, so he has $105.00 + $5.25 = $110.25. After another 6 months, his $110.25 has grown by $110.25 × 0.05 = $5.51 (rounded to the nearest cent), so he has $115.76. Finally, after another 6 months (2 years), his $115.76 has grown by $115.76 × 0.05 = $5.79 (rounded to the nearest cent), so he has $121.55.

——— Math 🌵 Camp ———
7

1 One quarter is worth $0.25, so 2 are worth $0.50. The chocolate bar costs $0.80, so your friend will have to loan you $0.80 − $0.50 = $0.30.

2 Students are instructed to a draw vertical number line (Fig. 69), labeled from 1,250 ft. to 1,300 ft. and showing their position at 1,290 ft.

3 The debt to the bank is $500 − $200 = $300.

4 Students are instructed to draw a vertical number line (Fig. 70). Descending from the ninth floor to the second floor means going down 9 − 2 = 7 floors. Each floor is 10 feet high, so student's figure should show the descent is 7 × 10 ft. = 70 ft.

5 Correct statements are − 29 < − 17 and − 17 > − 29. For the first, think "−29°F is less (colder) than −17°F." For the second, "−17°C is hotter (greater) than −29°C."

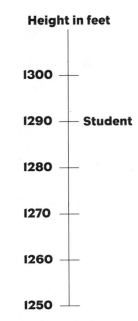

Figure 69 Math Camp 7, problem 2.

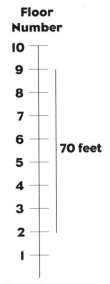

Figure 70 Math Camp 7, problem 4.

1 First there were 2 bunnies, 1 male and 1 female. Within 6 months, the female gave birth to 6 more bunnies, 3 male and 3 female. So after 6 months, you have 2 + 6 = 8 bunnies, 4 males and 4 females. Within the next 6 months, these 4 females each gave birth to 6 more bunnies, which adds 4 × 6 = 24 more bunnies. So after 12 months, you have 8 + 24 = 32 bunnies, 16 males and 16 females. Within the next 6 months, these 16 females each gave birth to 6 more bunnies, which adds 16 × 6 = 96 more bunnies. So after 18 months, you have 32 + 96 = 128 bunnies, 64 males and 64 females. Within the next 6 months, these 64 females each gave birth to to 6 more bunnies, which adds 64 × 6 = 384 more bunnies. So after 24 months, you have 128 + 384 = 512 bunnies. A table helps to organize the results and show the pattern, making it easier to see the answer after 4 years, which was given at the end of the problem.

Months	Bunnies
6	$8 = 2 \times 4$
12 (1 year)	$32 = 2 \times 4 \times 4$
18	$128 = 2 \times 4 \times 4 \times 4$
24 (2 years)	$512 = 2 \times 4 \times 4 \times 4 \times 4$
30	$2{,}048 = 2 \times 4 \times 4 \times 4 \times 4 \times 4$
36 (3 years)	$8{,}192 = 2 \times 4 \times 4 \times 4 \times 4 \times 4 \times 4$
42	$32{,}768 = 2 \times 4 \times 4 \times 4 \times 4 \times 4 \times 4 \times 4$
48 (4 years)	$131{,}072 = 2 \times 4 \times 4 \times 4 \times 4 \times 4 \times 4 \times 4 \times 4$

2 After 1 year, the bond is worth 1.06 x $10,000 = $10,600. After 2 years, the bond is worth 1.06 times the previous year's value, or 1.06 x $10,600 = 1.06 x (1.06 x $10,600) = (1.06 × 1.06) × $10,000 = $1.06^2 × $10,000 = $11,236. After 3 years, the bond is worth 1.06 times the previous year's value, or 1.06 x $11,236 = 1.06 x ((1.06 x 1.06) x $10,000) = (1.06 x 1.06 x 1.06) x $10,000 = $(1.06)^3 \times $10,000 = $11,910.16.

A table helps to organize the results and show the pattern.

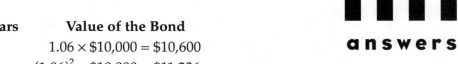

Age in Years	Value of the Bond
1	$1.06 \times \$10{,}000 = \$10{,}600$
2	$(1.06)^2 \times \$10{,}000 = \$11{,}236$
3	$(1.06)^3 \times \$10{,}000 = \$11{,}910.16$
4	$(1.06)^4 \times \$10{,}000 = \$12{,}624.77$
5	$(1.06)^5 \times \$10{,}000 = \$13{,}382.26$
…	…
…	…
…	…
18	$(1.06)^{18} \times \$10{,}000 = \$28{,}543.39$

3 John would need 8,388,608 cents = $83,886.08 for just the 24th square. The sum needed to cover all previous squares is always 1 cent less, or $83,886.07. The total would be $83,886.07 + $83,886.08 = $167,772.15. A table helps to organize the results and show the pattern. (The amount needed to cover the *entire* chessboard is gigantic.)

Chess Square	Number of Cents
1	$2^0 = 1$
2	$2^1 = 2$
3	$2^2 = 4$
4	$2^3 = 8$
5	$2^4 = 16$
6	$2^5 = 32$
…	…
…	…
23	$2^{22} = 4{,}194{,}304$
24	$2^{23} = 8{,}388{,}608$

4 [*Note to instructor:* This may be a challenging problem for some students, but it is worth the time needed to discuss and explain it.] At the end of the first week, there are $1 + 3 \times 1 = 4$ lotuses in the pond (the original 1 plus the 3 they produced). These 4 lotuses cover 8 sq. ft. One more is planted, making 5. At the end of the second week, these 5 have each produced 3 more, so there are $5 + 3 \times 5 = 20$ lotuses (5 plus the 15 they produced). These 20 lotuses cover 40 sq. ft. One more is planted, making 21. At the end of the third week, these 21 have each produced 3 more, so there are $21 + 3 \times 21 = 84$ lotuses. These 84 lotuses cover 168 sq. ft. One more is planted, making 85. At the end of the fourth week, these 85 have each produced 3 more, so there are $85 + 3 \times 85 = 340$

lotuses. These 340 lotuses cover 680 sq. ft. So it will take 4 weeks to cover the entire surface of the pond.

Math ⚜ Camp
9

1 The area of the 4-acre main square is $4 \times 43{,}560$ sq. ft. = 174,240 sq. ft. This is close to 417.42 ft. $\times$ 417.42 ft. = 174,239 sq. ft., so each side of the town square is about 417.42 ft. (to the nearest hundredth), or 417.4 ft. (to the nearest tenth).

2 10 ft. $\times$ 10 ft. $\times$ 10 ft. = 1,000 cu. ft., so each side is 10 ft.

3 0.5 in. $\times$ 0.5 in. $\times$ 0.5 in. = 0.125 cu. in., so each side is 0.5 in.

4 The long side of the rectangle is twice the short side. A rectangle having this shape and containing 30,000 sq. ft. is the same as two squares placed side by side, each square containing 15,000 sq. ft. Since 122.47 ft. $\times$ 122.47 ft. = 14,998.90 sq. ft. (to the nearest hundredth), the short side is about 122.47 ft. and the long side is about 244.94 ft.

Math ⚜ Camp
10

1 The ratio of the height of Mt. McKinley to that of Mt. Everest: $20{,}320/29{,}300 = 0.69$ (to the nearest hundredth) or 0.7 (to the nearest tenth).

2 Mary's to John's savings, as a fraction, is: $50/75 = (2 \times 25)/(3 \times 25) = 2/3 = 0.66666 \ldots$ or 0.67 (to the nearest hundredth), or 0.7 (to the nearest tenth).

3 John receives $(3/5) \times \$125 = \$75$ and Mary receives $(1/3) \times \$125 = \$41.67$ (to the nearest cent). The ratio of Mary's to John's gift: $(1/3)/(3/5) = (1/3) \times (5/3) = (1 \times 5)/(3 \times 3) = 5/9 = 0.5555 \ldots = 0.56$ (to the nearest hundredth). The sum of the two gifts is $\$75 + \$41.67 = \$116.67$.

4 Jules gave away 2/5: 1/5 to his brother, 1/5 to his sister. He is left with the other 3/5: 3/5 = 1/5 + 1/5 + 1/5. One of anything (in this case, the gift) is equal to 5/5, or 1/5 +1/5 + 1/5 +1/5 +1/5 = 5/5 = 1.

5 Mr. Gold gave a total of $100,000 × (10/100) = $10,000 to the charities. He gave (3/5) × $10,000 = $6,000 to the hospital, (1/4) × $10,000 = $2,500 to the Boy Scouts, and the rest, $10,000 − $6,000 − $2,500 = $1,500, to the homeless woman.

6 In dollars, George gave his sister (1/3) × $90 = $30, and his brother (1/4) × $90.00 = $22.50. This leaves $90.00 − $30.00 − $22.50 = $37.50 for George. As a fraction of his grandmother's gift, George is left with ($90.00 − $30.00 − $22.50)/$90.00, which is the same as 1 − 1/3 − 1/4 = 1 − 4/12 − 3/12 = 1 − 7/12 = 5/12.

7 As fractions, the total minority populations are 1/3 + 1/4 + 1/5 +1/6 = 20/60 + 15/60 + 12/60 + 10/60 = (20 + 15 + 12 + 10)/60 = 57/60 = (3 × 19)/(3 × 20) = 19/20. This is 0.95, or 95% of the town.

8 You spent (1/5) × $90 = $18 in January, (1/8) × $90 = $11.25 in February, and (1/6) × $90 = $15 in March. You spent a total of $18.00 + $11.25 + $15.00 = $44.25. This leaves $90.00 − $44.25 = $45.75 in the account. After adding $30.00 in April, the account contained $75.75. As a fraction, this is 75.75/90 = 0.8416666 . . ., or 0.84 (to the nearest hundredth). Another way in terms of fractions: 1 − 1/5 − 1/8 − 1/6 + 1/3 = 120/120 − 24/120 − 15/120 − 20/120 + 40/120 = 101/120 = 0.8416666 . . . , or about 84% of the original amount.

9 The winner takes 3 hr. = 180 min.; the winner's speed is 500/180 = 2.7777 . . . , or 2.8 mi./min. (to the nearest tenth). The second-place winner takes 3 hr. 15 min. = 195 min.; her speed is 500/195 = 2.6 mi./min. The third-place winner takes 3 hr. 20 min. = 200 min.; his speed is 500/200 = 2.5 mi./min. The ratio of the second-place winner's speed to the first-place winner's is 2.6/2.8 = 0.93 (to the nearest hundredth). The ratio of the third-place winner's speed to the first's is 2.5/2.8 = 0.89. The ratio of the third-place winner's speed to the second's is 2.5/2.6 = 0.96.

answers

10 In pounds, the total is $1/2 + 4/5 + (1 + 1/3) + 2 = 15/30 + 24/30 + 30/30 + 10/30 + 60/30 = (15 + 24 + 30 + 10 + 60)/30 = 139/30 = 4 + 19/30$.

11 For the second car, the discount is 12%, or $20,000 × (12/100) = $2,400, so this car costs $20,000 − $2,400 = $17,600. For the third car, the discount is $21,000 × (15/100) = $3,150, so this car costs $21,000 − $3,150 = $17,850. For the fourth car, the discount is $19,000 × (7/100) = $1,330, so that car costs $19,000 − $1,330 = $17,670. The second car is the cheapest. The first car is the most expensive.

12 The ratio is $45,000/60,000 = 45/60 = (3 × 15)/(4 × 15) = 3/4$, which is 0.75.

13 Since 27 cu. ft. = 3 ft. × 3 ft. × 3 ft., the first cube has a side of 3 ft. And since 64 cu. ft. = 4 ft. × 4 ft. × 4 ft., the second cube has a side of 4 ft. The ratio of the sides is $3/4 = 0.75$.

——————— Math 🌿 Camp ———————

11

1 **a)** $(+\$20) + (+\$20) + (+\$20) + (+\$20) = +\$80$. You are now $80 richer.

b) $(-\$15) + (-\$15) + (-\$15) + (-\$15) = -\$60$. You are now $60 poorer.

c) $(+\$20) \times (-3) = -\$60$. Three weeks ago, you were $60 poorer.

d) $(-\$25) \times (-4) = +\$100$. Four weeks ago, you were $100 richer.

2 $(-\$10) \times (+3) + (+\$25) = (-\$30) + (+\$25) = -\$5$. You lost $5.

3 $(+10°F) + (+21) \times (-5°F) = (+10°F) + (-105°F) = -95°F$. This is $(5/9) \times (-95°F - 32°F) = -70.6°C$ (rounded to the nearest tenth of a degree centigrade).

4 $(-10°C) + (+5) \times (+3°C) = (-10°C) + (+15°C) = +5°C$. Two days ago, the temperature was 5°C above the freezing point of water.

5 If all the apples had been good, the cost per apple would have been $15/45 = $1/3 = $0.33333 . . . = 33.3 cents per apple (to the nearest tenth of a cent). Because 10 apples were rotten, the amount of money wasted was 10×33.3 cents = $3.33 (to the nearest cent). The cost of each good apple was $15/35 = $0.428571 . . . = $0.43 = 43 cents (to the nearest cent).

6 The temperature went down $(+20°C) - (-10°C) = +30°C$ in 7 days, so the temperature went down an average of $(+30°C)/7$ or 4.3°C per day (to the nearest tenth of a degree).

7 The stock went down $150 - $110 = $40 in 7 days. So the average change in stock value was a loss of $40/7 = $5.71 per day (to the nearest cent).

8 Let "sea level" be the zero point, let "above sea level" be plus, and let "below sea level" be minus. Then Mt. Everest is +29,300 feet and the deepest point in the Indian Ocean is −33,300 feet. So the vertical distance between the top of Mt. Everest and the bottom of the Indian Ocean is $(+29,300) - (-33,300) = +62,600$ feet (or about 11.9 mi., to the nearest tenth of a mile).

9 The store paid $1,000 \times $30 = $30,000 for the shoes. The store sold 750 pairs at $50 and the remaining 250 at $25, for a total of: $750 \times $50 + 250 \times $25 = $37,500 + $6,250 = $43,750$. So the store made a profit of $43,750 - $30,000 = $13,750 on 1,000 pairs of shoes, or $13,750/1,000 = $13.75 per pair of shoes.

10 John's account of $1,000 earns 5% annual interest, so after 2 years it would be worth $(1.05) \times (1.05) \times ($1,000) = $1,102.50$. Because he borrowed $750 at 10% annual interest for 2 years from the bank, John must repay $(1.10) \times (1.10) \times ($750) = 907.50 to the bank. The amount left in his account is the difference: $1,102.50 - $907.50 = $195. [Instructors might point out that if John had taken the $750 from his bank account, the remaining $250 would have earned 5% annually. Then the amount in his account after 2 years would have been $(1.05) \times (1.05) \times ($250) = 275.63 (to the nearest cent), which is $275.63 - $195.00 = $80.63 more. The added money is due to the fact that he avoids paying interest of 5% on $750 for 2 years.]

11

$$1,724,265 = 1.724265 \times 10^6$$
$$245.572 = 2.45572 \times 10^2$$
$$0.00275 = 2.75 \times 10^{-3}$$
$$0.000000022 = 2.2 \times 10^{-8}$$
$$0.000000000003 = 3 \times 10^{-12}$$

12

$$2.75 \times 10^4 = 27,500$$
$$6.125 \times 10^6 = 6,125,000$$
$$200.25 \times 10^5 = 20,025,000$$
$$2.3 \times 10^{-2} = 0.023$$
$$1.45 \times 10^{-3} = 0.00145$$
$$-4.5 \times 10^{-2} = -0.045$$

13 $1.05^{10} \times \$200 = 1.6288\ldots \times \$200 = \$3.25778\ldots \times 10^{-2} = \$325.78$ (to the nearest cent).

14 4.5×10^9 yr. = 4,500,000,000 yr., or four billion, five hundred million years.

15 15 billion yr. = 15,000,000,000 yr. = 1.5×10^{10} yr.

16 $2 \times 60 \times 60$ sec. = 7,200 sec. = 7.2×10^3 sec.
$1/(60 \times 60)$ hr. = 0.00027777 $\ldots$ hr. = 2.78×10^{-4} hr. (rounded).

17 $14,000,000,000 \times 365$ days = 5,110,000,000,000 days = 5.11×10^{12} days.

18 $4,500,000,000 \times 365 \times 24$ hr. = 39,420,000,000,000 hr. = 3.942×10^{13} hr.

——— Math 🔥 Camp ———
12

(The operation of rounding is indicated here by the arrow →)

1 Rounded off to the nearest hundred: 576 → 600; 9,460 → 9,500; 10,097 → 10,100; 110,452 → 110,500; 1,000,890 → 1,000,900; 2,445,667,224 → 2,445,667,200

2 Rounded off to the nearest hundred thousand:
1,095,022 → 1,100,000; 10,897,252 → 10,900,000;
2,999,754 → 3,000,000; 1,002,003,004 → 1,002,000,000

3 The sixth-grade class has 32 + 30 + 34 + 31 = 127 students.
The seventh-grade class has 33 + 32 + 30 + 34 + 32 = 161
students. The eighth-grade class has 35 + 39 + 25 = 99 students. The total number of students in school is 127 + 161 +
99 = 387. Rounded to the nearest hundred: 387 → 400.

4 The total population of the six states is 12,348,693 →
12,000,000 to the nearest million.

5 Rounding the six populations to the nearest million and
then adding produces: 3,000,000 + 1,000,000 + 6,000,000 +
1,000,000 + 1,000,000 + 1,000,000 = 13,000,000. The difference (due to adding then rounding instead of rounding
then adding) is 1,000,000.

—————— Math  Camp ——————
13

1 The answer depends on the length of the student's arm.

2 The answer depends on the length of the student's average
step.

3 The height of the building is 50 × 9 ft. = 450 ft. = 150 yd.

4 The area is 100 ft. × 150 ft. = 15,000 sq. ft. = 1,666.7 sq. yd.

5 The cube's volume is $(0.63 \text{ ft.})^3 = 0.25$ cu. ft. This is 12 × 12 ×
12 × 0.25 = 432 cu. in.

6 85°F is the same as 5/9 × (85°F − 32°F) = 29.4°C or 29°C (to
the nearest degree).

7 Water boils at 212°F and freezes at 32°F.

8 12 minutes is 12/60 = 0.2 hr., so the total running time is
2.2 hr. The average speed is 26.2/2.2 = 11.9 in mph.
Since 1 mi. = 5,280 ft., and 1 hr. = 3,600 sec., we have

1 mph = 5,280/3,600 = 1.47 ft./sec. So the runner's average speed is 11.9 × 1.47 = 17.5 ft./sec.

9 The average speed is 3,000/4.5 = 666.7 mph or 666.7 × 1.47 = 980 ft./sec. (See previous problem for the conversion factor of 1.47.)

10 The radius of the pipe is 1 ft., so the volume of the pipe is 3.14 × 100 = 314 cu. ft. The number of seconds in a day is 60 × 60 × 24 = 86,400 sec. The water flows at 1 ft./sec. or 86,400 ft./day. The area through which it flows is 3.14 sq. ft. The water flow in cubic feet per day is 3.14 sq. ft. × 86,400 ft./day = 2.71×10^5 cu. ft./day.

11 50°F = 10°C and 20°F = – 6.7°C. The rate of change of temperature was (50°F – 20°F)/12 hr. = 2.5°F/hr. This is [10°C – (–6.7°C)]/12 hr. = 1.4°C/hr.

12 90°C = 194°F and 40°C = 104°F. The average rate of temperature change in 30 minutes is (194°F – 104°F)/30 min. = 3°F/min.

13 The volume of concrete is 100 ft. × 3 ft. × 4 ft. = 1,200 cu. ft. This is 1,200/27 cu. yd. At $300/cu. yd., the cost is $300 × (1,200/27) = $13,333.33.

14 From problem 7, water boils at 100°C and freezes at 0°C. To calculate Kelvin degrees from centigrade degrees, K = C – (–273) = C + 273. So water boils at 373°K and freezes at 273°K.

15 Since there are 60 seconds in a minute, 1,000 seconds is the same as 1,000/60=16.67 minutes (rounded to nearest hundredth). Although a year is about 365.25 days long (which is why we have a leap year every 4 years), we will round this number and assume 365 days in a year. (Using 365.25 won't change your answer very much. Try it.) Since the number of hours in a century is 100 × 365 × 24 = 876,000 (not far from 1 million), 1 million hours is the same as 1,000,000/876,000 = 1.14 centuries (to the nearest hundredth). After you read about prefixes in Section 2, you'll understand why 1 kilosecond equals 16.67 minutes and 1 megahour equals 1.14 centuries.

——————— Math ⚜ Camp ———————

14

1 & 2 The student's answers to these problems are estimates in SI units. Answers will vary from student to student, but they should be reasonable approximations to the answers given for problems 1 and 2 in Math Camp 13.

3 From Math Camp 13, the building height is 450 ft. In meters, this is $450 \times 0,305 = 137,25$ m or 137 m (to the nearest meter).

4 One side is 100 ft. In meters, this is $100 \times 0,305 = 30,5$ m. The other side is 150 ft., which in meters is $150 \times 0,305 = 45,75$ m. The area is: $30,5$ m $\times 45,75$ m $= 1\,395,375$ m^2. In dekameters, $30,5$ m $= 3,05$ dam. The area is $3,05$ dam $\times 4,575$ dam $= 13,953\,75$ dam^2.

5 The cube's edge is 12 in., so its volume is 12 in. $\times$ 12 in. $\times$ 12 in. $= 1,728$ cu. in. From the table of conversion factors, this is $1\,728 \times 16,387 = 28\,317$ (rounded off to nearest cubic meter, m^3). Since 1 m $= 100$ cm, 1 m$^3 = 1\,000\,000$, so the volume in cubic meters is $28\,317 / 1\,000\,000 = 0,028\,317$ m^3.

6 Converting Fahrenheit to centigrade, 50°F is $5/9 \times (50°F - 32°F) = 10°C$.

7 From Math Camp 13, the average speed of the marathon winner is 11.9 mi./hr., or 17.5 ft/sec. This is $11,9 \times 1,609 = 19,1$ km/hr. (nearest tenth of a km/hr.), or $17,5 \times 0,305 = 5,34$ m/s (rounded to the nearest hundredth m/s).

8 From the table of conversion factors, 1 mi. $= 1,609$ km. So 3,000 mi. is $3\,000 \times 1,609 = 4\,827$ km. Thus the plane's average speed, in 6 hr., is $4\,827 / 6 = 804,5$ km/hr. This is the same as $804\,500$ m/hr. Since 1 hr. $= 3,600$ s, the average speed is $804\,500 / 3,600 = 223,5$ m/s.

9 From Math Camp 13, the water flow is $2.71 \cdot 10^5$ cu. ft. From the table of conversion factors, 1 cu. ft. equals $0,028\,3$ m^3. The water flow is $2,71 \times 10^5 \times 0,028\,3 = 7\,669$ m^3/day. A liter (l) is a cubic decimeter $= 1/1000$ m^3. The water flow is $7\,669\,000$ l/day.

10 From Math Camp 13, the cost of the concrete is $13,333.33. At 1 500 lire to the dollar, this is $13,333.33 × (1 500 lire/$) = 20 000 000 lire.

──────── Math ⚜ Camp ────────
15

(In the following, π is approximated as 3.14.)

1 **a)** The lake contains 3.14 × 50 × 50 × 4 = 31,400 cu. ft. of water.

b) The inside of the circular path is 3.14 × 2 × 50 = 314 ft.

c) The outside of the circular path is 3.14 × 2 × 54 = 339 ft. (to the nearest foot).

2 **a)** The 25 inner columns on either side stand on a quarter circle, an arc of 90°, and they are equally spaced, which means the angle between two adjacent columns is 1/24 of this arc or 90/24 = 3.75°.

b) The area is 3.14 × 300 × 300 = 282,600 sq. ft.

c) The length of one inner row of columns is 1/4 the circumference of the inner circle, which is 0.25 × 2 × 3.14 × 300 = 471 ft.

d) The length of one outer row of columns is 1/4 the circumference of the outer circle, which is 0.25 × 2 × 3.14 × 360 = 565.2 ft.

3 If the diameter of a porthole is 1.5 ft., the radius is 0.75 ft., and the area is 3.14 × 0.75 × 0.75 = 1.8 sq. ft. (to the nearest tenth).

4 The radius of the carousel, including the wooden platform, is 22 ft., so the area occupied by the carousel is 3.14 × 22 × 22 = 1,520 sq. ft. (to the nearest sq. ft.).

5 The Chunnel's diameter is 2 × 70 = 140 ft. and its length is 30 × 5,280 ft. = 158,400 ft. The Chunnel's surface area is 3.14 × 140 × 158,400 sq. ft. = 69,632,640 sq. ft.

6 The area of the side is 3.14 × 3 × 4.5 = 42.39 sq. in. The area of each end is (1/4) × 3.14 × 3 × 3 = 7.065 sq. in. The number of square inches of tin needed to build the can is 42.39 + 2 × 7.065 = 56.52 sq. in.

7 Using successive approximations, the area of a circle with a radius of 4 in. is $3.14 \times 4 \times 4 = 50$ sq. in. (to the nearest sq. in.). So the diameter of the cooking pot is 8 in. (to the nearest in.).

8 The pool contains $3.14 \times 10 \times 10 \times 6 = 1{,}884$ cu. ft. of water.

9 Example: The student's wrist measurement shows a circumference of 8 in. Assuming the wrist has a circular cross section, the diameter is $8/3.14 = 2.54$ in. (to the nearest hundredth). So the radius is $2.54/2 = 1.27$ in., and the area is $3.14 \times 1.27 \times 1.27 = 5$ sq. in. (to the nearest sq. in.).

10 Radii $36°$ apart divide a circle into $360/36 = 10$ equal parts. Radii $51.43°$ apart divide a circle into $360/51.43 = 7$ equal parts (to the nearest integer).

11 The student is instructed to throw toothpicks of length L on a piece of paper with parallel lines spaced the same distance, L, apart. Calculate R, the ratio of the number of toothpicks that cross a line, to the total number of toothpicks thrown. The ratio $2/R$ approaches 3.14 as the number of thrown toothpicks increases. (This is Buffon's needle problem, as recast by Laplace; see *A History of Pi* by Petr Beckmann, 1971.)

—————— Math 🌿 Camp ——————
16

1 The third angle is $180° - 35° - 60° = 85°$.

2 The third angle is $180° - 2 \times 45° = 90°$.

3 The third side is
$\sqrt{7^2 + 7^2} = \sqrt{98} = 9.89\ldots = 10$ in. (to the nearest inch).

4 The height is 3 in. [The height to the base forms two right triangles, each being 3, 4, 5 (each hypotenuse is 5 in.; one side, being half the base, is 4 in.; the other side is the height, which is common to the two right triangles).] The perimeter is $5 + 5 + 8 = 18$ in. The semiperimeter is 9 in. The isosceles triangle's area is $(1/2) \times 8 \times 3 = 12$ sq. in.

5 The diagonals are
$$\sqrt{8.5^2 + 11^2} = \sqrt{72.25 + 121} = \sqrt{193.25} = 13.9 \text{ in.}$$
(to the nearest tenth).

6 A diagonal is $\sqrt{100^2 + 100^2} = \sqrt{20,000} = 141.4 \text{ ft.}$
(to the nearest tenth).

7 Draw the height to the base. The facade is two right triangles, each having a leg of 25 ft. and a hypotenuse of 60 ft. The height is the third side, which is:
$$\sqrt{60^2 - 25^2} = \sqrt{3,600 - 625} = \sqrt{2,975} = 54.54 \text{ ft.}$$
The facade's area is: $(1/2) \times 50 \times 54.54 = 1,363.5$ sq. ft.

8 The top of the ladder is
$$\sqrt{6^2 - 4^2} = \sqrt{20} = 4.47 \text{ ft.}$$
(to the nearest hundredth) above the floor.

9 The triangle's hypotenuse is
$$\sqrt{6^2 + 4^2} = \sqrt{52} = 7.2 \text{ in.}$$
(to the nearest tenth). Its area is $1/2 \times 4 \times 6 = 12$ sq. in.

10 The bracket is a right triangle. The inclined side is the hypotenuse, whose length is
$$\sqrt{2^2 + 2.5^2} = \sqrt{10.25} = 3.2 \text{ ft.}$$
(to the nearest tenth).

Math Camp
17

1 The business district has a perimeter of 2×90 ft. + 2×120 ft. = 420 ft. Its area is 90 ft. $\times$ 120 ft. = 10,800 sq. ft.

2 The town square's perimeter is 4×40 ft. = 160 ft. Its area is 40 ft. $\times$ 40 ft. = 1,600 sq. ft. The length of its diagonal is
$$\sqrt{40^2 + 40^2} = 56.56 \text{ ft.}$$
(to the nearest hundredth).

3 The perimeter is 2×100 ft. + 2×80 ft. = 360 ft. The area is 100 ft. $\times$ 60 ft. = 6,000 sq. ft.

4 [The answer is $4 \times 4 = 16$ sq. in., but we calculate the area the hard way.] Draw a diagonal. The square is made of two identical right triangles. The length of the diagonal $\sqrt{4^2 + 4^2} = 5.66$ in. (to the nearest hundredth). From the hint, the other diagonal is perpendicular and has the same length, so the height of one of the triangles is $1/2$ the diagonal, or $5.66/2 = 2.83$ in. The area of this triangle is $(b \times h)/2 = (5.66 \times 2.83)/2 = 8.01$ sq. in. (to the nearest hundredth). There are two identical triangles, so the area of the square is $2 \times 8.01 = 16.02$ sq. in.

5 The area of a parallelogram is equal to the area of a rectangle of the same base and height. (To show this, pick up the right triangle from one side and move it to the other side, making the rectangle.) The base is 9 in. and the height is 4 in., so the area is $9 \times 4 = 36$ sq. in. A square with the same area must have a side of $\sqrt{36} = 6$ in.

6 The quadrilateral's perimeter is $5 + 5 + 12 + 12 = 34$ in. The quadrilateral is made of two identical right triangles, $5^2 + 12^2 = 13^2$. Each triangle's area is $(5 \times 12)/2 = 30$ sq. in., so the area of the quadrilateral is $2 \times 30 = 60$ sq. in.

7 The quadrilateral's perimeter is $8 + 17 + 9 + 12 = 46$ in. The quadrilateral is made of two right triangles, $8^2 + 15^2 = 17^2$ and $9^2 + 12^2 = 15^2$. The area of the first triangle is $(8 \times 15)/2 = 60$ sq. in. and the area of the second is $(9 \times 12)/2 = 54$ sq. in., so the quadrilateral's area is $60 + 54 = 114$ sq. in.

—————— Math 🌾 Camp ——————
18

1 The student is instructed to draw 6 circles and inscribe 6 regular polygons (see problem 2 below).

2 The student is instructed to measure the side of each regular polygon in problem 1. Entries in the last column of the table (next page) were computed to the nearest hundredth using trigonometry. Students will not get such accurate answers from their drawings. However, the asymptotic trend toward $\pi \cong 3.14$ should be clear. If not, the student should be instructed to repeat his or her work more carefully.

Inscribed regular polygon	Number of sides N	Perimeter divided by diameter
triangle	3	2.60
square	4	2.83
pentagon	5	2.94
hexagon	6	3.00
octagon	8	3.06
dodecagon	12	3.09

3 The hexagon consists of 6 equilateral triangles, each side being equal to the radius of the circle, 2 in. Each equilateral triangle consists of 2 right triangles. The hypotenuse of these right triangles equals 2 in. and one leg equals 1 in. The length of the other leg of the right triangles is the height of the equilateral triangles, $\sqrt{2^2 - 1^2} = \sqrt{3} = 1.73$ in. (to the nearest hundredth). The area of 1 equilateral triangle is $1/2 \times 2 \times 1.73 = 1.73$ sq. in., so the area of the hexagon is $6 \times 1.73 = 10.38$ sq. in. The side of a square with the same area as the hexagon is $\sqrt{10.38} = 3.22$ in.

4 The area of the rectangle is $2 \times 8 = 16$ sq. ft. The side of a square with the same area as the rectangle is $\sqrt{16} = 4$ ft.

Math Camp
19

(In the following, π is approximated as 3.14.)

1, 2 &3 In the following table, the radii are numbers given in the text. The results under Volume and Area are obtained by rounding off the answers to the last figure given.

problem	radius (approx.)	volume	surface area
1) earth	4,000 mi.	2.7×10^{11} cu. mi.	2×10^{8} sq. mi.
2) sun	432,000 mi.	3.4×10^{17} cu. mi.	2.3×10^{12} sq. mi.
3) a. basketball	5 in.	523 cu. in.	314 sq. in.
b. soccer ball	4.25 in.	321.4 cu. in.	226.9 sq. in.
c. tennis ball	1.25 in.	8.2 cu. in.	19.6 sq. in.

4 The column's vertical surface area is $S = 4 \times 15 = 60$ sq. ft. The column's circumference is 4 ft., so its radius is $4/(2 \times 3.14) = 0.637$ ft. (rounded off to nearest last figure), and its volume is $V = 3.14 \times (0.637)^2 \times 15 = 19.1$ cu. ft.

5 The area of one of the prism's rectangular faces is $1/2$ in. $\times 10$ in. $= 5$ sq. in. The area of one of its triangular bases is $1/2 \times 1/2 \times (1/2 \times \sqrt{3}/2) = 1.732/16 = 0.108$ sq. in. The total area of the three faces plus two bases $= 3 \times 15 + 2 \times 0.108 = 45.2$ sq. in. (rounded off to the nearest tenth).

———— Math Camp ————
20

1, 2, 3, 4 & 5
The student constructs five Platonic solids.

6 The student checks Euler's characteristic relation: $f + v = e + 2$.

polyhedron	faces	vertices	edges
tetrahedron	4	4	6
hexahedron	6	8	12
octahedron	8	6	12
dodecahedron	12	20	30
icosahedron	20	12	30

1

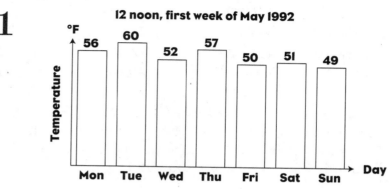

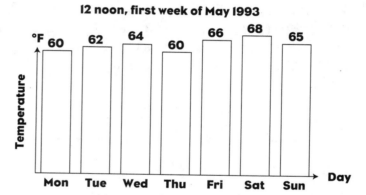

Figure 71 Math Camp 21, problem 1.

2

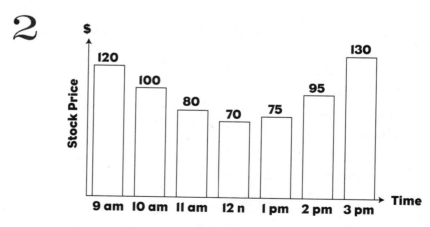

Figure 72 Math Camp 21, problem 2.

3

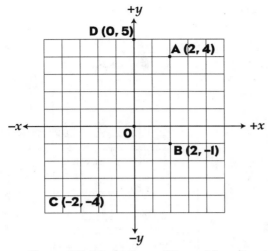

Figure 73 Math Camp 21, problem 3.

4

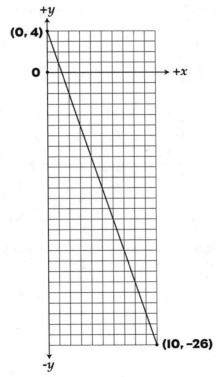

Figure 74 Math Camp 21, problem 4.

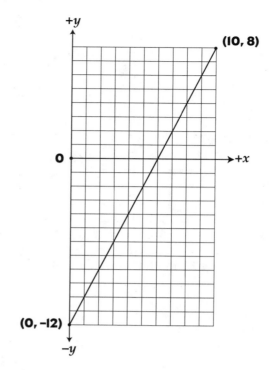

Figure 75 Math Camp 21, problem 5.

6

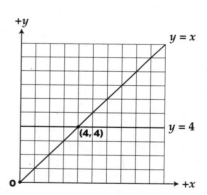

Figure 76 Math Camp 21, problem 6.
The two lines intersect at $x = 4$, $y = 4$.

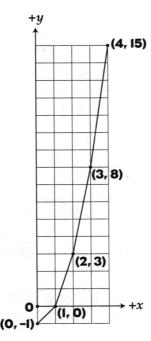

Figure 77 Math Camp 21, problem 7.

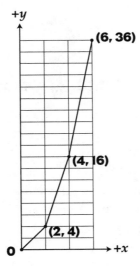

Figure 78 Math Camp 21, problem 8.

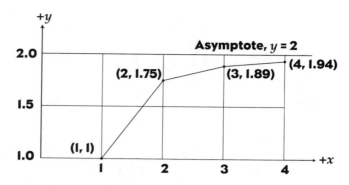

Figure 79 Math Camp 21, problem 9. (Some values were rounded to nearest hundredth.)

10 Drawing of living room by student.

11 The top of the Leaning Tower of Pisa leans out $\sqrt{180^2 - 179^2} = \sqrt{359} = 18.9$ ft. (to the nearest tenth) above the edge of its base.

12-15 Sketches, to scale, by students.

———— Math 🌵 Camp ————
22

1
$$10x + 10y = \$5.00 \qquad (1)$$
$$5x + 12y = \$3.90 \qquad (2)$$

Make the coefficient of y the same in both equations by multiplying all coefficients of equation (1) by 6/5.
$$12x + 12y = \$6.00 \qquad (3)$$
$$5x + 12y = \$3.90 \qquad (2)$$

Subtract equation (2) from equation (3) to get $7x = \$2.10$, from which $x = \$2.10/7 = \$0.30$. Substitute this into equation (1): $10 \times \$0.30 + 10y = \$5.00$ or $\$3.00 + 10y = \$5.00$ or $10y = \$5.00 - \$3.00 = \$2.00$ or $y = \$2.00/10 = \$0.20$.

2 $x = 3, y = 3.$

3 Add 24 to both sides of $3x - 24 = 12$ and get $3x = 36$. Divide both sides by 3 and get $x = 12$. Substitute $x = 12$ into the second equation and get $(-3)(12) + y = 10$ or $-36 + y = 10$; add 36 to both sides and get $y = 46$.

4 Add the equations and get $24x = 24$. Divide both sides by 24 and get $x = 1$. Subtract the second equation from the first and get $8y = 8$; divide both sides by 8 and get $y = 1$.

5 Let x be the price of 1 bottle of French wine and y be the price of 1 bottle of California wine.

$$1x + 2y = \$35. \tag{1}$$
$$2x + 2y = \$50. \tag{2}$$

Subtract equation (1) from equation (2): $x = \$15$. Substitute into equation (1):

$\$15 + 2y = \$35$ or $2y = \$35 - \$15 = \$20$ or $y = \$20/2 = \$10$.

So 1 bottle of French wine costs \$15 and one bottle of California wine costs \$10.

6 Let x be the price of 1 chocolate bar and y be the price of 1 Coke.

$$2x + 1y = \$1.00 \tag{1}$$
$$1x + 2y = \$1.25 \tag{2}$$

Make the coefficient of x the same in both equations by multiplying both sides of equation (2) by 2.

$$2x + 1y = \$1.00 \tag{1}$$
$$2x + 4y = \$2.50 \tag{3}$$

Subtract equation (1) from equation (3): $3y = \$1.50$ or $y = \$1.50/3 = \$0.50$. Substitute into equation (2): $1x + (2 \times \$0.50) = \$1.25$ or $x + \$1.00 = \$1.25$ or $x = \$1.25 - \$1.00 = \$0.25$.

So 1 chocolate bar costs \$0.25 and 1 Coke costs \$0.50.

7 Let x be the number of lire that \$1 can buy (lire/\$), and y be the number of lire that 1 German mark (DM) can buy (lire/DM).

$$\$500x + 200y = 1{,}200{,}000 \tag{1}$$

$$\$100x + 300y = 760{,}000 \tag{2}$$

Make the coefficient of x the same in both equations by multiplying both sides of equation (2) by 5.

$$\$500x + 200y = 1{,}200{,}000 \tag{1}$$

$$\$500x + 1{,}500y = 3{,}800{,}000 \tag{3}$$

Subtract equation (1) from equation (2): $1{,}300y = 2{,}600{,}000$ or $y = 2{,}600{,}000/1{,}300 = 2{,}000$ lire/DM. Substitute into equation (1): $\$500x + (200 \times 2{,}000) = 1{,}200{,}000$ or $\$500x + 400{,}000 = 1{,}200{,}000$ or $\$500x = 1{,}200{,}000 - 400{,}000 = 800{,}000$ or $x = 800{,}000/\$500 = 1{,}600$ lire/\$.

8 Let x be the cost of 1 gallon of gas, and y be the cost of 1 quart of oil.

$$10x + 2y = \$19.60 \tag{1}$$

$$13x + 1y = \$20.20 \tag{2}$$

Make the coefficient of y the same in both equations by multiplying all coefficients of equation (2) by 2.

$$10x + 2y = \$19.60 \tag{1}$$

$$26x + 2y = \$40.40 \tag{3}$$

Subtract equation (1) from equation (2): $16x = \$20.80$ or $x = \$20.80/16 = \$1.30$.

Substitute into equation (2): $(13 \times \$1.30) + y = \$20.20$ or $\$16.90 + y = \$20.20$ or $y = \$20.20 - \$16.90 = \$3.30$.

So 1 gallon of gas costs \$1.30 and 1 quart of oil costs \$3.30.

9 Let x be the number of masons, and y be the number of apprentices. At one building, the rate of pay is $72 per mason per day, and $40 per apprentice per day. In dollars per day, we know $72x + 40y = \$2,040$. At the other building, the rate of pay is $80 per mason per day, and $48 per apprentice per day. In dollars per day, we know $80x + 48y = \$2,320$.

$$72x + 40y = 2,040 \qquad\qquad (1)$$
$$80x + 48y = 2,320 \qquad\qquad (2)$$

Make the coefficient of x the same in both equations by multiplying all coefficients of equation (2) by $9/10 = 0.9$.

$$72x + 40y = 2,040 \qquad\qquad (1)$$
$$72x + 43.2y = 2,088 \qquad\qquad (3)$$

Subtract equation (1) from equation (3): $3.2y = 48$ or $y = 48/3.2 = 15$. Substitute into equation (1): $72x + (40 \times 15) = 2,040$ or $72x = 2,040 - 600 = 1,440$ or $x = 1,440/72 = 20$.

10 Let x be the weight of the coffee selling for $4.70 a pound, and y be the weight of the coffee selling for $2.70 a pound. The total weight of coffee in one pound is made up of x plus y, or $x + y = 1$. And the cost of the mixture, in dollars, must be $4.70x + 2.70y = 3.70$.

$$1x + 1y = 1 \qquad\qquad (1)$$
$$4.70x + 2.70y = 3.70 \qquad\qquad (2)$$

Make the coefficient of x the same in both equations by multiplying all coefficients of equation (1) by 4.70.

$$4.70x + 4.70y = 4.70 \qquad\qquad (3)$$
$$4.70x + 2.70y = 3.70 \qquad\qquad (2)$$

Subtract equation (2) from equation (3): $2.00y = 1.00$ or $y = 1.00/2.00 = 1/2$. Substituting into equation (1): $x + 1/2 = 1$ or $x = 1 - 1/2 = 1/2$. In other words, mix equal amounts of the two kinds of coffee.

11 Let x be the number of parents who bought tickets at \$1, and let y be the number of students who bought tickets at 50 cents = \$ 0.50. The total number of tickets sold is 200 so $x + y = 200$. The amount collected is \$150 so, in dollars, $1x + 0.50y = 150$.

$$x + y = 200 \tag{1}$$
$$x + 0.5y = 150 \tag{2}$$

Subtract equation (2) from equation (1): $0.5y = 50$ or $y = 50/0.5 = 100$. Substitute into equation (1): $x + 100 = 200$ or $x = 200 - 100 = 100$. In other words, the same number of students and parents bought tickets.

12 Let x be the number of \$20 bills, and y be the number of \$50 bills. The total number of bills is 35, so $x + y = 35$. The amount is \$1,000, so $20x + 50y = 1,000$ (in dollars).

$$1x + 1y = 35 \tag{1}$$
$$20x + 50y = 1,000 \tag{2}$$

Make the coefficient of x the same in both equations by multiplying all coefficients of equation (1) by 20.

$$20x + 20y = 700 \tag{3}$$
$$20x + 50y = 1,000 \tag{2}$$

Subtract equation (3) from equation (2): $30y = 300$ or $y = 300/30 = 10$. Substitute into equation (1): $x + 10 = 35$ or $x = 35 - 10 = 25$.

— Math ☀ Camp —
23

1 Assume the friends are standing beside one another and you are looking at the photograph. The friend on the left is one of five different people, the friend in the middle is one of the remaining four, and the friend on the right is one of the remaining three. So the number of different photographs is $5 \times 4 \times 3 = 60$. This is the same as the number of permutations of 5 different things taken 3 at a time, which is $P(5,3) = 5!/2! = 60$ possible photographs.

2 Though the table is square, this is a "circular" permutation (assuming orientation of the table in the room is ignored). The number of circular permutations of 4 things is $(4-1)! = 3! = 6$. Another way is to start counting from some person, indicating that person by X. Any one of three remaining diners may sit on X's left, any of two remaining diners may sit on X's right, and the one remaining diner sits across from X. So the number of possible ways the 4 people can be seated is $3 \times 2 \times 1 = 6$ ways.

3 A team is 4 players, without regard to order, taken from the 10 aspirants. This is the number of combinations of 10 things taken 4 at a time, or $C(10,4) = 10! / (4! \times 6!) = (10 \times 9 \times 8 \times 7)/(4 \times 3 \times 2 \times 1) = 10 \times 3 \times 7 = 210$ possible teams of 4 players from among the 10 aspiring players.

4 A "mixed doubles" team means a female–male partnership. In the trials, male player 1 could be a partner to any of the 5 female players. Male player 2 could also be a partner to any of the 5 female players. The same is true for male players 3, 4, and 5. So the total number of possible female-male partnerships is $5 \times 5 \times 5 \times 5 \times 5 = 5^5 = 3{,}125$.

5 The menu has 5 courses with each course offering 2 items. The first course can be either of 2 possibilities, the second can be either of 2 possibilities, the third can be either of 2, and so forth. The number of different dinners possible is $2 \times 2 \times 2 \times 2 \times 2 = 2^5 = 32$.

6 Call the seats 1 through 8, starting with the left-most seat on one side of the compartment. Any one of the 8 travelers can sit in seat 1, one of the remaining 7 in seat 2, and so forth. The number of possibilities is $8 \times 7 \times 6 \times \ldots \times 1 = 8! = 40{,}320$. This is also the "number of permutations of 8 things taken 8 at a time," $P(8,8) = 8! / (8{-}8)! = 8!/0! = 8!$, where $0! = 1$ has been used. Students should realize that this problem is, for counting purposes, the same as the problem of seating 8 students in a classroom with 8 chairs. They should then realize that, with 8 seats and 6 travelers, this is the same as the classroom with 8 chairs and 6 students, $P(8,6) = 8!/2! = 20{,}160$. Reviewing a game of musical chairs and talking about compartment seats moving around while the travelers stay put might help.

7 Jane may choose the first pair of shoes from one of 10 different pairs, and then she may choose the second pair from one of the 9 remaining pairs, which is $10 \times 9 = 90$ different ways. However, Jane does not care which of these two pairs is called the first and which is called the second. In other words, switch the pairs around and the purchase is the same two pairs. So the answer is 1/2 of 90 or 45 possible pairs. A faster way of counting is to notice, before starting to count, that the order of choosing pairs that fit does not matter in the final purchase. So we want the number of combinations of 10 pairs taken 2 pairs at a time or $C(10,2) = 10!/(8! \times 2!) = 45$ pairs.

8 Painting A is one of 6 different paintings. Painting B is one of the remaining 5 paintings. Painting C is one of the remaining 4. Continue this way until Painting F is the one remaining painting, which is $6 \times 5 \times 4 \times 3 \times 2 \times 1 = 6! = 720$ different arrangements. This is the same as the linear permutation of all 6 paintings or 6!. This is also the same as the (linear) permutation of 6 paintings, taken all 6 at a time, or $P(6,6) = 6!/0! = 6! = 720$.

9 The number of possible ways to make up one group of books is equal to the number of combinations of 9 books taken 3 at a time, $C(9,3) = 9!/(6! \times 3!) = (9 \times 8 \times 7)/(3 \times 2 \times 1) = 84$. The number of possible ways to make up the next group is the number of combinations of the remaining 6 books taken 3 at a time, $C(6,3) = 6!/(3! \times 3!) = (6 \times 5 \times 4)/(3 \times 2 \times 1) = 5 \times 4 = 20$ ways. The last group is made up of the remaining 3 books taken 3 at a time, $C(3,3) = 1$. The total number of ways is the product of these three combinations, $84 \times 20 \times 1 = 1,680$.

10 Look at any two socks. Sock 1 is one of the 12 socks in the drawer. Sock 2 may then be of the remaining 11, which is a total of $12 \times 11 = 132$ possibilities. Since it does not matter which is called sock 1 and which is called sock 2, we must have counted each pair twice. In other words, switch the socks around and we have the same pair. So the number is 1/2 of 132 or 66 possible pairs. A faster way is to notice, before starting to count ordered arrangements, that the order of the two socks does not matter in the final pair of socks (the grays are identical). So we want the number of combinations of 12 things taken 2 at a time, $C(12,2) = 12!/(10! \times 2!) = 66$.

11 Encourage the student to think about whether this is a problem in permutations or combinations. Presumably the order of invitations (or other orderings such as which of the two friends arrives first at the birthday party) should not be important in counting the number of ways two friends are invited to the party. The student can then see that this is a problem in combinations. The count is the same as the number of combinations of 5 things taken 2 at a time, $C(5,2) = 5!/(3! \times 2!) = 10$. (If it does matter who is invited first and second, then there are twice as many possibilities.)

——————— Math ⚘ Camp ———————
24

1 & 2 1 and 2 are student projects.

3 The probability of getting a specific sequence in 5 throws, such as HHHHH = 5 Hs, is $1/2 \times 1/2 \times 1/2 \times 1/2 \times 1/2 = (1/2)^5 = 1/32 = 0.03125$, or about 3%. The probability of getting 10 Hs (or any other specific sequence in 10 throws) is $(1/2)^{10} = 1/1{,}024 = 0.000976$, which is near 0.001, or about 1 in 1,000 throws. Similarly, the probability of getting 20 Hs (or any other specific sequence in 20 throws) is $(1/2)^{20} = (1/2)^{10} \times 1/2^{10} = (1/1{,}024) \times (1/1{,}024) = 9.54 \times 10^{-7}$, which is near 0.000001, or about 1 in a million throws. The probability of getting 1 more H after each of the preceding sequences is $1/2$, independent of the preceding sequence.

4 The probability of getting 5 Ts followed by 5 Hs (or any other specific sequence) is $(1/2)^5 \times (1/2)^5 = 1/2^{10}$, or about 1 in 1,000 throws. The probability of an H after any sequence is $1/2$, regardless of what the sequence is or how long it is.

5 The probability of guessing the first number is 1 out of 50 or $1/50$. The probability of guessing the third number is also $1/50$. The probability of guessing both numbers is the product of the separate probabilities, $(1/50) \times (1/50) = 1/2{,}500 = 0.0004$. The probability of guessing any two numbers is the same, $(1/50) \times (1/50) = 1/2{,}500 = 0.0004$.

6 The probability of the first extracted ball matching one of your 6 numbers is 6 out of 50 or 6/50. Extracted balls are not returned to the urn, so only 49 balls remain. The probability of one of your remaining 5 numbers matching one of the remaining 49 balls is 5 out of 49 or 5/49. Then the probability of one of your remaining 4 numbers matching one of the remaining 48 balls is 4/48; then 3/47, 2/46, 1/45. The probability of matching all 6 numbers is the product, $(6/50) \times (5/49) \times (4/48) \times (3/47) \times (2/46) \times (1/45) = (6 \times 5 \times 4 \times 3 \times 2 \times 1)/(50 \times 49 \times 48 \times 47 \times 46 \times 45) = 720/11,441,304,000 = 1/15,890,700 = 6.3 \times 10^{-8}$. The probability of winning this lotto is only a little bit better than winning the other one, where balls are put back in the urn before the next ball is extracted.

7 The probability of guessing the first extracted ball is 1 out of 10 or 1/10. Because extracted balls are put back in the urn before the next ball is withdrawn, the probability of guessing the second ball is the same as the first, 1/10. The probability of hitting the jackpot by guessing both is the product, $(1/10) \times (1/10) = 1/100$ or 1 out of 100.

8 The probability of these two events is the product of the separate probabilities, $(1/2) \times (1/6) = 1/12$, or, on average, 1 of 12 times when the penny and die are thrown simultaneously.

9 You believe your chance of winning both tournaments is $(9/10) \times (8/10) = 72/100$.

10 The letters are disregarded in this problem. The only plates with 3 equal numbers are 000, 111, 222, 333, ..., 888, or 999, which is a total of 10 plates. There are $10^3 = 1,000$ possible plates. So the probability of a standard car plate having 3 equal numbers is $10/(10)^3 = 1/(10 \times 10) = 1/100$, or 1 in 100 plates.

11 The numbers are disregarded in this problem. The only plates with 3 equal letters are AAA, BBB, CCC ... YYY, or ZZZ, which is a total of 26 plates. There are $(26)^3 = 17,576$ possible plates. So the probability is $26/(26)^3 = 1/(26 \times 26) = 1/676 = 0.00145$, or less than 15 out of every 10,000 plates.

12 The first number is one of 10 numbers, the second number is one of the remaining 9 numbers, the third number is one of the remaining 8 numbers. Similarly, the first letter is one of 26 letters, the second letter is one of 25 letters, and the third letter is one of 24 letters. So the total number of possible plates with all different numbers and all different letters is $10 \times 9 \times 8 \times 26 \times 25 \times 24$. The total number of plates with all possible combinations of numbers and letters is $(10)^3 \times (26)^3$. So the probability of a standard car plate having all different numbers and all different letters is $(10 \times 9 \times 8 \times 26 \times 25 \times 24)/(10)^3 \times 26^3 = (9/10) \times (8/10) \times (25/26) \times (24/26) = 0.639$, or about 64 out of 100 plates, which is less than two-thirds of all plates.

13 The number of plates with all equal numbers and all equal letters is 10×26, because 000 is with AAA, BBB . . . or ZZZ; 111 is with AAA, BBB . . . or ZZZ; . . . 999 is with AAA, BBB . . . or ZZZ. The total number of plates with all possible combinations of numbers and letters is $(10)^3 \times 26^3$. So the probability of a standard car plate having all equal numbers and all equal letters is $(10 \times 26)/(10)^3 \times (26)^3 = (1/100) \times (1/676) = 0.0000145$, or less than 15 out of every 1 million plates. Another way to obtain this result is to note that it is the product of the probabilities found in problems 10 and 11 above.

14 [The probability of shooting two 1s—or two particular numbers on two dice—is the same as the probability of throwing 2 on the top face of die A and 5 on the top face of die B, discussed in Section 4 of Chapter Ten, on Shooting Craps.] The probability of shooting a 1 on the first die is 1 out of 6, or $1/6$, and the probability of a 1 on the second die is also $1/6$. Hence the probability of this particular event is $(1/6) \times (1/6) = 1/36$ or, on average, 1 in 36 throws of the dice.

15 There are six numbers on a die and three of them are even: 2, 4, and 6. So the probability of throwing an even number on one die is $3/6 = 1/2$. Hence the probability of throwing two even numbers is $(1/2) \times (1/2) = 1/4$, or 1 in 4 throws of the dice.

16 One die may show any number. The probability that the other die matches is 1 out of 6, or $1/6$.

Index

A
abstract ideas, 2
addition, 11–12
    of fractions, 33–35
    of negative numbers, 39–40
addition symbol, 11
algebra, 89
algorithms, 30
angles, 62
Arabic numerals, 3
Archimedes, 60, 95–96
area, 50, 58
    See also formulas
asymptotic approach, 95–96

B
bar graphs, 89–90
base, triangle, 70
bases, number system, 5, 7–8
Bhaskara, 4–5
binary number system, 7–8
British measurement system, 50, 56

C
calculus, 82
Cartesian coordinates, 91
Cartesian plane, 90–94
centigrade degrees, 24–25
centigrade to Fahrenheit conversion, 49
centimeters, 53
Central America, 4–5
certainty, 119
chance. See probability
Chunnel, 64
circles
    dividing into quadrants, 61
    drawing, 58–59
    measuring, 59–61
    terms used to describe, 57–58
    used in graphs, 62–63
circular graphs, 62–63
circular permutations, 108–9
circumference, 58
coefficients, 103–4
columns, 81
combinations, 112–14
combination symbol, 113
common denominators, finding, 34–36
commutative property, 11, 14
computers, 7–8
conversion factors, British to SI units, 56

coordinates, 91
counting, 2–3
counting symbols, 3–5
craps, 124–26
cube roots, 30
cube root symbol, 30
cubes, 85
cubic meters, 53
cubing numbers, 26–27
curved line graphs, 93–95
cylinders, 81

D
decimal dot, 4
decimal number system, 4–5, 7–8, 27
decimeters, 53
degrees symbol, 61
dekameters, 53
denominator, 32
Descartes, René, 26, 89–90
diagonals, 73
diameter, 58
difference, 16
digits, 1
distance measurement, 50
dividend, 18
division, 18–20
    of fractions, 36, 37
    of negative numbers, 41
division symbols, 18–19
divisor, 18
dodecagons, 76
dodecahedron, regular, 86–87
dot
    decimal, 4
    multiplication symbol, 13–14

E
equal sign, 16
equations, 16
equilateral triangles, 66–67, 84–85, 86, 87–88
estimating, 44–45
Euler, Leonard, 88
Everest, Mount, 37, 43
exponential symbols, 5, 26–27, 41–42
exponents, 5, 26–27

F
Fahrenheit degrees, 17–18
Fahrenheit to centigrade conversion, 49

Fermat, Pierre de, 69
Fermat's last theorem, 69
fluxions, theory of, 82
force, 50, 53
formulas
    area, 26, 61, 70–71, 74
    British to SI units conversion, 56
    circumference, 61
    surface area, 80
    temperature conversion, 49
    volume, 27, 80, 81, 82
fractions, 32–33
    adding, 33–35
    common denominators, 34–36
    in decimal form, 33
    dividing, 36, 37
    multiplying, 33–35, 36–37
    roots of, 37
    subtracting, 35–36
fraction symbols, 32
France, 52

G
geometry
    definition of, 57
    influence of Greeks, 59–60, 67–69, 71,
        83–84, 95–96
    See also plane geometry; space geome-
        try
graphs
    bar, 89–90
    for calculating pi, 95–96
    in the Cartesian plane, 90–94
    curved line, 93–95
    drawn to scale, 97–98
    straight line, 90–93
Greece, 59–60, 67–69, 71, 83, 84, 95–96

H
height, triangle, 70
Heron's formula, 71
Hero's formula, 71
hexagons, 76
hexahedron, regular, 85
Hindu-Arabic numerals, 3–5
Hindus, 4–5
history of math, 1–5
hypotenuse, 67–68

I
icosahedron, regular, 87–88
India, 4–5
Indian Ocean, 43
inscribing polygons, 76–77
integers, 68
International System, 52
intersection point, 93
irrational numbers, 59
isosceles triangles, 66–67, 70–71

J
Japanese numerals, 3

K
Kelvin degrees, 52
Khowarizmi, al-, 30
kilograms, 53
kilometers, 53

L
Leaning Tower of Pisa, 100
least common denominators, 36
Leibniz, Gottfried Wilhelm von, 82
less than symbol, 19
license-plates, 122–23
linear equations, 103–4
linear equations, simultaneous, 92–93,
    103–4
linear permutations, 107–8, 110–12, 114–16
liters, 53
lotto, 122

M
mass, 53
Mayas, 4–5
McKinley, Mount, 37
measuring, 49
measuring systems, 50, 52–54
meters, 52
metrication, 52
metric conversion formulas, 56
metric system, 52
millimeters, 53
minuend, 16
minus sign, 16, 39, 41–42
modern metric system, 52
more than symbol, 19
multiplicand, 14
multiplication, 13–14
    of fractions, 33–35, 36–37
    of negative numbers, 41
multiplication principle, 109
multiplication symbols, 13–14
multiplication table, 15
multiplier, 14

N
Napoleon, 52
negative numbers, 23–25
    adding, 39–40
    dividing, 41
    multiplying, 41
    subtracting, 39–40
Newton, Isaac, 82
newtons, 53
n factorial, 108
n factorial symbols, 108, 110
number lines, 23–25, 40–41, 90
numbers, invention of, 1–5
numerals, 3–5

numerator, 32

O

octagons, 76
octahedron, regular, 86
operational value, 23–25, 39
origin, 23, 90

P

parallelograms, 73
penny throwing, 119–21
pentagons, 76, 86–87
percent symbol, 19
perimeter, 71, 73
permutations, circular, 108–9
permutations, linear, 107–8, 110–12, 114–16
permutation symbol, 111
pi, 59–61, 95–96
pipes, 81
Pisa, Leaning Tower of, 100
plane geometry
    circles, 57–63
    quadrilaterals, 73–74
    regular polygons, 76–77
    triangles, 66–71
Plato, 84
Platonic solids, 83–84
plus sign, 11, 39, 41–42
polygons, 66
positional value, 23–25, 39
positive numbers, 23–25
prisms, 81–82
probability
    certainty, 119
    in craps, 124–26
    in license plates, 122–23
    in lotto, 122
    in penny throws, 119–21
    theory, 119–20
product, 14
protractors, 62
pyramids, 84
Pythagoras, 67–69
Pythagorean theorem, 67–69

Q

quadrants, 61
quadratic equations, 71
quadrilaterals, 73–74
quotient, 18

R

radius, 57–58
ratio, 32
rectangles, 73
rectangular prisms, 81
regular dodecahedron, 86–87
regular hexahedron, 85
regular icosahedron, 87–88
regular octahedron, 86

regular polygons, 66, 76–77
regular tetrahedron, 84–85
remainder, 19
rhombuses, 73
right triangles, 67–69
roots, 29–31
roots, extracting, 30
root symbol, 30
rounding off, 45–46

S

scale, drawing to, 97–98
scalene triangles, 66
Science Museum of Paris, 52
semiperimeter, 71
Shanks, William, 60
shooting craps, 124–26
shorthand symbols, 3–5
simultaneous linear equations, 92–93,
    103–4
SI (Système international) measurement
    system
    conversion factors, 56
    getting used to, 54–55
    history of, 52
    prefixes, 54
    rules for writing in, 54
    symbols, 53–54
    units, 52–53
space geometry
    cylinders, 81
    dimensions of space, 79
    polyhedra, 83–88
    prisms, 81–82
    spheres, 79–80
    torus, 80
spheres, 79–80
square meters, 53
square prisms, 81
square roots, 30
square root symbol, 30
squares, 73, 85
squaring numbers, 26, 29
St. Peter's Church, 64
straight line graphs, 90
subtraction, 15–17
    of fractions, 35–36
    of negative numbers, 39–40
subtraction symbol, 16
subtrahend, 16
successive approximations, 30
sums, 11–12
symbols
    addition, 11
    almost equal to, 55
    combination, 113
    counting, 3–5
    cube root, 30
    degree, 61
    division, 18–19

equal sign, 16
exponential, 5, 26–27, 41–42
fraction, 32
less than, 19
minus sign, 11, 39, 41–42
more than, 19
multiplication, 13–14
n factorial, 108, 110
percent, 20
permutation, 111
pi, 59
plus sign, 11, 39, 41–42
root, 30
SI unit, 53–54
square root, 30
subtraction, 16
Système international (SI), 52

T
Taylor, Richard, 69
temperature measurement, 17–18, 24–25, 49
tetrahedron, regular, 84–85
torus, 80
trapezoids, 73
triangles
    equilateral, 66–67, 84–85, 86, 87–88
    isosceles, 66–67, 70–71
    measuring, 69–71
    right, 67–69
    scalene, 66

triangular prisms, 82
trigonometry, 71
Tsu Ch'ung-chih, 60

U
units of measurement, 49
unknowns, 15

V
Verrazano Narrows Bridge, 101
vertices, 70
volume, 50
    See also formulas

W
Washington, George, 52
weight, 53
Wiles, Andrew, 69
World Trade Center, 21

X
x-axis, 90
x-coordinate, 91

Y
y-axis, 90
y-coordinate, 91

Z
zero, 4–5

ALSO AVAILABLE

Math Games and Activities from Around the World

Multicultural fun for ages 8 to 12
Claudia Zaslavsky
160 pages, 11 x 8½
10 b & w photos, line drawings throughout
paper, $14.95 ISBN 1-55652-287-8

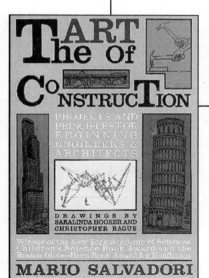

The Art of Construction

Projects and Principles for Beginning Engineers and Architects
Mario Salvadori
ages 10 and up
160 pages, 7 x 10
illustrated throughout
paper, $12.95 ISBN 1-55652-080-8

CHICAGO REVIEW PRESS

Both books are available at your favorite bookstore or from Independent Publishers Group, 814 N. Franklin St., Chicago, IL 60610, 312-337-0747 or 1-800-888-4741, or ipgbook@mcs.com